Batsford Chess Library

Winning With the Kan

Ali Mortazavi

An Owl Book
Henry Holt and Company
New York

Henry Holt and Company, Inc.
Publishers since 1866
115 West 18th Street
New York, New York 10011

Henry Holt® is a registered
trademark of Henry Holt and Company, Inc.

Published in Canada by Fitzhenry & Whiteside Ltd.,
195 Allstate Parkway, Markham, Ontario L3R 4T8.

First published in the United States in 1996 by
Henry Holt and Company, Inc.
Originally published in Great Britain in 1996 by
B. T. Batsford Ltd.

Library of Congress Catalog Card Number: 95-81558

ISBN 0-8050-4724-7 (An Owl Book: pbk.)

First American Edition—1996

Printed in the United Kingdom
All first editions are printed on acid-free paper.∞

10   9   8   7   6   5   4   3   2   1

Editorial Panel: Mark Dvoretsky, John Nunn, Jon Speelman
General Adviser: Raymond Keene OBE
Commissioning Editor: Graham Burgess

Contents

Symbols

+	Check
++	Double check
x	Capture
!!	Excellent move
!	Good move
!?	Interesting move
?!	Dubious move
?	Bad move
??	Blunder
±±	White is winning
±	White is much better
±	White is slightly better
=	Equal position
∓	Black is slightly better
∓	Black is much better
∓∓	Black is winning
OL	Olympiad
Ch	Championship
Cht	Team Championship
Wch	World Championship
Z	Zonal
IZ	Interzonal
Ct	Candidate event
jr	Junior event
wom	Women's event
mem	Memorial event
sim	Simultaneous game
rpd	Rapidplay game
corr.	Postal game
(n)	nth match game
(D)	Diagram follows

Bibliography

Books

Winning with the Sicilian, Taimanov (Batsford 1990)
Sicilian: Paulsen, Taimanov (Batsford 1984)
Beating the Sicilian 2, Nunn (Batsford 1990)
My Best Games, Karpov (RHM 1978)
Secrets of Grandmaster Play, Nunn & Griffiths (Batsford 1987)

Periodicals

Informator
ChessBase Magazine
New in Chess

Introduction

In my chess-playing career, I have examined many openings and attempted to incorporate them into my repertoire. Partly due to sheer laziness and partly due to time limitations, I was simply not able to learn all the relevant lines and as a result had to endure many needless losses to weaker players simply through lack of opening knowledge. The main problem was that I was always trying to improvise in opening systems that had been deeply analysed – and so improvisation was nearly impossible.

When a friend showed me the bare outlines of the Sicilian Kan, the system looked like any other Sicilian and I again resigned myself to more losses. However, on further inspection, with the use of *ChessBase* databases and other reference material, I noticed that very few people actually played this line on a regular basis. Moreover, theory books had dismissed the opening as a non-starter, giving convincing lines for White only. It still took many humiliations by various friends in blitz games to make me realise that

there really was something to be said for what seemed like a kind of 'gap' in chess opening theory.

One of the most encouraging signs was that whenever I mentioned the name 'Sicilian Kan', the usual response was "What's that? You mean the Taimanov?". In fact the Kan Variation is widely known as the Paulsen Variation. However, most Sicilian experts played the Paulsen Variation as if it were a Taimanov Sicilian. This, as we shall see, is a fundamental error, as one of the main ideas of the Kan is to delay ...♘c6 (a typical Taimanov move) unless one can play it in favourable circumstances.

Having now played the system for three years, I have yet to find a single book that gives the best lines for Black. There is so much preoccupation now with the Najdorf Sicilian and the infamous Poisoned Pawn Variation that the rest of the Sicilian variations have taken a back seat. However, the Classical Variation, the Taimanov and even the Kan are creeping into top-class chess as more and more players realise their merits. I cannot claim that Kan gives Black an advantage but I do guarantee a sound system with the added bonus of allowing room for creativity and improvisation.

Some of the games that are analysed (especially in the Hedgehog formation) arise from a Taimanov move order but they nevertheless still demonstrate the basic strategy of the Kan due to the similarity between the two variations.

Why the Sicilian?

Before we progress to a discussion of specific lines, I would like to present a case for the Sicilian Defence in general, without prejudice for particular variations.

In my opinion, every serious chess player should have experience of the main lines of the Open Sicilian. The reason behind this is that after Black has exchanged his flank pawn for one of White's central pawns, we reach a unique pawn structure which has the potential to incorporate all of the fundamental facets of chess strategy. No other opening is so rich in sacrificial ideas, mating formations, pawn storms and tactical nuances. In addition to the tactical possibilities, the opening

also contains strategic concepts such as overprotection, backward pawns, the positional sacrifice, etc.

In short, whatever variation of the Sicilian you adopt, there is a beneficial side effect for your general chess ability.

The Basic Kan

1 e4 c5 2 ♘f3 e6 3 d4 cxd4 4 ♘xd4 a6 *(D)*

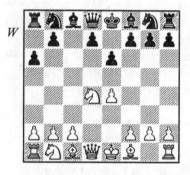

In the above position, Black has just played 4...a6, signifying his intention to play the Kan Variation of the Sicilian. One striking feature of the above diagram is that Black has not developed any of his minor pieces. In the Najdorf and Dragon variations, Black develops his king's knight and in the Taimanov the b8-knight is developed. One of the main ideas of the Kan is the slight delay in the development of the minor pieces. The reason for this phenomenon is that Black is waiting to see what formation White chooses before committing himself to his own structure. The Taimanov Variation gives us an early example of how White can gain a slight concession when Black shows his cards early:

1 e4 c5 2 ♘f3 e6 3 d4 cxd4 4 ♘xd4 ♘c6 5 ♘b5 d6 6 c4 ♘f6 7 ♘1c3 a6 8 ♘a3 ♗e7 9 ♗e2 and here one of the main moves for Black is to play the slightly paradoxical 9...♘b8. The justification for this knight retreat lies in the fact that the knight is badly placed on c6 when White has adopted the Maroczy Bind (pawns on e4 and c4). For example, let's see what happens if Black were to continue his development in classical fashion, e.g. 9...0-0 10 0-0 b6 11 ♗e3 ♗b7 12 ♖c1 ♕c7?! (D).

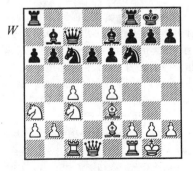

Then after 13 ♘d5! exd5 (forced; otherwise White wins material) 14 cxd5 White regains the piece with a big structural advantage.

The Kan move-order, by contrast, does not commit the knight and may thereby save a whole move. It should be noted, however, that the loss of this tempo is not too serious and 9...♘b8 in the Taimanov is a perfectly playable system.

One other delaying mechanism that Black uses in the Kan is playing ...d6 as late as possible. Nearly always the queen is placed on c7 where it exerts some influence along the semi-open c-file but more importantly, the queen controls the b8-h2 diagonal. One of the main reasons that Black delays ...d6 is that some of the cruder mating ideas based on ...♕c7, ...♘f6-g4 and, ...h5 are no longer possible when this diagonal is closed. In addition, the queen stalls White's e4-e5 ideas. In general, Black only plays ...d6 when White forces him to, by threatening e4-e5 with a preparatory f2-f4 or ♕d1-e2. If White cannot play e5, then Black is more than happy to keep this diagonal open for as long as possible.

Another beneficial effect of delaying ...d6 is that the black bishop on f8 has a choice of squares along the diagonal rather than being forced to go to e7. Indeed, the ability to play ...♝c5 is one of the main ideas in the Kan.

White's systems

An attractive feature of this opening is the limit on the number of systems that White can employ. In the Najdorf, for example, Black has to meet systems with ♝c4 (the Fischer-Sozin), ♝g5, f2-f4, a2-a4, ♝e3 (the English Attack), etc. In this Sicilian, Black realistically only has to know three different set-ups:

1) The Hedgehog formation;
2) Scheveningen-style positions;
3) g3 systems.

Of these, the first is the most popular and the third is rarely met but can be quite dangerous if Black is caught napping.

The Maroczy Bind and Hedgehog formations

The Maroczy Bind describes a pawn formation which was initially thought to give White a big advantage due to its restricting nature. Typically, players who

allowed this pawn formation were often faced with a cramped position and minor pieces rarely ventured past the third rank. The following diagram shows the basic Maroczy Bind *(D)*:

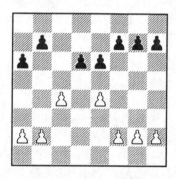

It is apparent from the diagram that with the aid of his minor pieces, White can minimise (and at best completely nullify) all of Black's possible pawn breaks. Meanwhile, Black huddles deep inside his camp, adopting the Hedgehog formation and waits for an opportune tactical moment to break out with ...d5 or ...b5.

At this stage, the reader might well wonder what the advantage of playing such a passive system is? Perhaps the most important point is that, given that the onus is on White to pursue his first move advantage, Black sets up a pawn formation which is extremely hard to break down, even though it is slightly passive. Indeed, one of the features of the Hedgehog formation is that the position is far harder for White to convert than for Black to defend. Black's moment typically arrives when White loses patience and takes his eye off the d5- and b5-squares.

If such a moment does arrive, Black is comforted by the fact that the pawn breaks ...b5 and especially ...d5 usually have a devastating effect as all of Black's pieces are liberated in one stroke.

The first chapter features a full discussion of the Hedgehog system, and the methods that typify it.

Scheveningen-style positions

The Scheveningen is yet another variation of the Sicilian which was a favourite of Garry Kasparov until he finally settled on the Najdorf. The defence has a slightly passive look as Black plays both ...e6 and ...d6 and allows White to develop at will.

The diagram below is a typical Scheveningen position. Many experts have dismissed the Kan as a bad version of the Scheveningen because Black allows White to play his light-squared

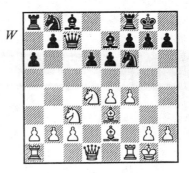

bishop to d3 (1 c4 c5 2 ♘f3 e6 3 d4 cxd4 4 ♘xd4 a6 5 ♗d3) where it menacingly eyes the h7-pawn. However, as we shall see, the opening makes up for this concession with its flexibility.

Others

If you play the Sicilian Defence, you will have noticed that learning all the main lines can sometimes be a fruitless experience. Many players are so put off by the supposed myriad of complications in the main line that they head for the less turbulent waters of the g3 systems.

Although these systems are not without their respective ideas (indeed some of the best players in the world have occasionally used them), Black, backed up with some 'do's and don'ts' should have no trouble in equalising.

1 Maroczy Bind and Hedgehog formations

The Hedgehog is a name given to a pawn formation adopted by Black against another pawn formation, the Maroczy Bind, which is adopted by White.

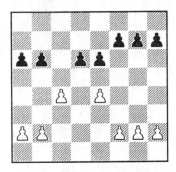

The above diagram is a typical pawn structure depicting the Maroczy Bind and the Hedgehog. White's pawn formation is known as a bind due to the restricting nature of the c4- and e4-pawns, which deny Black the necessary pawn breaks to liberate his position.

From the diagram, White's advantages are obvious. The pawns are used to cramp Black's position and as a result White can very often boast a clear spatial advantage. In addition to this, White can also pressurise Black's weak d-pawn along the semi-open d-file.

At first sight, there is very little to shout about in Black's own structure. His pawns are undeniably weaker than White's and his position is cramped. However, in practice, Black's structure holds up so well that it has been named after an animal that uses its coat as its main source of defence. Although White can usually keep Black's activity to a minimum, he will find it extremely hard to breach the third-rank defence that Black has built up. However, the minute White extends himself in a bid for victory, Black is more than capable of defending himself and many a strong player has found that the Hedgehog is one of the toughest defences to crack.

In many respects, the Hedgehog is the perfect 'black' structure. Black accepts his disadvantage and seemingly huddles behind a wall of pawns. In doing this, he puts the onus firmly on White to prove his first move advantage but is nonetheless poised to defend himself as actively as possible. In grandmaster chess, this scenario is really the best Black can ever hope for. Of course, White may simply do nothing and play for a draw but at that level, players are very reluctant to waste the advantage of the first move. For lesser players, I would say that the Hedgehog is as good a winning try as any other defence. One of the hardest things in chess is to do nothing without losing control over your position.

The d5-square

The diagram on the previous page shows that one of Black's main pawn breaks in the Hedgehog formations is by playing ...d6-d5 at an opportune moment. Unfortunately, an 'opportune moment' is hard to describe in simple text but we can gain some knowledge from Nimzowitsch's concept of 'overprotection'.

In his famous book, *My System*, Nimzowitsch outlined the principle that just as we defend our pieces from attack, protection of individual squares is just as important a concept. In fact, he went slightly further than simple pro-

tection and coined the term 'overprotection', denoting the need to protect a particular square with more than just one piece. By this, Nimzowitsch claimed that the player who overprotects, gains certain benefits from the position. The following diagram is an example of White overprotecting d5 in comparison to Black's 'underprotection' (D):

Here, White is protecting (albeit indirectly in some cases) d5 with: pawns on c4 and e4, knights on c3 and e3, queen on d2, rook on d1 and the bishop on g2. Black, on the other hand, has only three pieces protecting the same square: the knight on f6, the bishop on b7 and the pawn on e6. Thus from the above diagram, we can deduce that White has a spatial advantage and for the time being he has nullified Black's counter-attacking chances.

For Black to have any chance of playing the liberating ...d6-d5, he must have more protection over d5 than White. A general rule of thumb is that if Black does manage to 'secure' the d5-square for himself, then the position can be considered as equal or even slightly in Black's favour. The reason for this is that a 'successful' ...d5 liberates all of Black's seemingly passive pieces in one stroke. Often the rooks are activated, the bishops on b7 and e7 have open diagonals and the knights are centralised. If the above diagram is an ideal scenario for White, then the next one resembles what Black should be aiming for *(D)*:

Here, the roles have been reversed. Black has five pieces that directly or indirectly cover d5 compared to White's three. Therefore we can deduce that this is an 'opportune' moment to

break out with 1...d5!. In addition to the liberation of Black's pieces, note how a successful ...d5, as in the above diagram, puts White in a very difficult position. Black's threats are numerous; the immediate threat is simply to win White's e-pawn. However, if White plays 2 exd5?! after 2...exd5, he has inadvertently created an indirect attack on his queen on e2 by the black rook on e8. If the queen just vacates e2, Black could then simply play ...dxc4 and have a clear advantage.

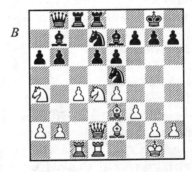

From the above diagram, in A.Sokolov-Lautier, Manila IZ 1990, Black found a novel way to promote the ...d5 thrust: 1...♖c7!? 2 b3 ♗a8 3 ♘c3 ♘f6 4 ♕b2 ♖cd7! 5 b4 d5! 6 cxd5 exd5 7 exd5 ♘xd5 8 ♘xd5 ♖xd5 9 ♘f5 ♗f6 10 ♖xd5 ♗xd5 and Black had completely nullified White's advantage.

Occasionally, Black plays ...d5 as a pawn sacrifice when White has weakened his kingside.

In this position, the veteran Korchnoi played the slightly ambitious 1 g4?! to which Black countered 1...♘e5 2 ♘g2 d5! 3 cxd5 ♗c5! when Black clearly had good play for the pawn.

The ...b5 break

The previous example of the successful ...d5 break by Black shows us that the Maroczy Bind pawn formation can be undermined. In addition to ...d5, Black can also attempt to undermine the bind by breaking on the queenside with ...b5. This break is similar to ...d5 in that it challenges White's pawn structure, but on its own, rarely achieves much more. Black's pieces are no more or less liberated and the only beneficial consequence is that one of White's d5 defenders is removed.

Indeed, it is fair to say that ...b5 is often played as a preparatory measure to play ...d5 as White's protection of the d5-square is lessened.

In general, White is much more likely to allow Black to play ...b5 than ...d5. The main reasons for this have been outlined in the previous paragraph but in addition to these, White himself can occasionally benefit from ...b5.

Here, Black has enough pieces covering b5 to play 1...b5?. However, after 2 axb5 axb5 3 ♘b4!, White gains a large advantage. In this precise position, White in fact wins a pawn by force after 3 ♘b4!. In general, however, a knight on b4 that cannot be dislodged by a black pawn is also an advantage in its own right.

We can also see that by playing ...b5, Black weakens certain squares on the queenside, in particular a5. Black will do well to refrain from ...b5 until he is sure that these two possibilities will not be advantageous for White.

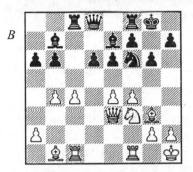

In this position, 1...b5! is a viable option as White has no way to take advantage of the queenside weaknesses created by this move. By contrast, Black's advantages in playing 1...b5, are both immediate and long-term. The immediate effects include use of the a-file, the lessening of the vice-like grip of the Maroczy Bind and a less cramped position. In the long term, Black can use c4-square for his pieces, e.g. via the manoeuvre ...♘f6-d7-b6-c4.

Again, in the diagram below, White has no means by which to infiltrate on the queenside and therefore Black played 1...b5!. The game Nunn-J.Horvath, Lucerne Wcht 1989, continued 2 cxb5 axb5 3 b4 d5! 4 ♕f2 (4 exd5 exd5 and Black is attacking the queen on e2 and threatening ...d4)

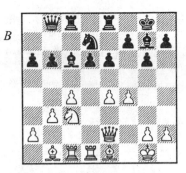

4...♘b6! 5 e5 ♘c4! and Black's slightly cramped position was fully compensated by his massive knight on c4.

The Fischer Attack

We have covered the more traditional plans for Black in the Hedgehog. The next idea is a formation first seen in the games of Bobby Fischer which Black players now regularly use as an alternative plan to the previous sections.

Although both games begin as a Sicilian Taimanov, Black reverts to the Kan set-up, bringing the queen's knight from c6 to the preferred d7-square.

Game 1
I.Gurevich-Zsu.Polgar
New York 1992

1 e4 c5 2 ♘f3 e6 3 d4 cxd4 4 ♘xd4 ♘c6 5 ♘b5 d6 6 c4 ♘f6 7 ♘1c3 a6 8 ♘a3 b6 9 ♗e2 ♗b7

10 0-0 ♘b8 11 f3 ♘bd7 12 ♗f4
♕c7 13 ♕d2 ♗e7 14 ♖fd1 ♘e5
15 ♖ac1 0-0 16 ♗e3 ♖ac8 17
♔h1 *(D)*

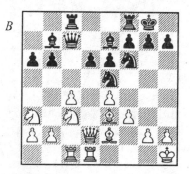

Here, we have a standard
Hedgehog formation with the
difference that the opening was
actually a Sicilian Taimanov
rather than a Kan. Nevertheless,
the only noticeable difference is
the slightly misplaced white
knight on a3, which is usually
placed on d4 in the Kan. Anyway,
White nearly always retreats the
knight from d4 to c2 in the Kan
to pressurise the d6-pawn and the
same principle is applied in the
Taimanov.

Although the moves so far have
been fairly routine, White has
made the decision to bolster his
e-pawn with f2-f3 rather than
adopting the more aggressive f2-
f4 formation. This set-up was
first popularised by Grandmaster

Lev Polugaevsky who instead of
simply attacking Black on the
kingside with f4, adopted the
more restrained approach of se-
curing the centre and playing on
the queenside.

If Black were to adopt the
standard Hedgehog approach of
doing nothing, White would follow up with the simple plan of
♘a3-c2, ♕e1-f2 in conjunction
with queenside expansion. As an
antidote to this system, Black has
begun to employ what has become to be known as the Fischer
plan, which constitutes an ambitious kingside attack.

17...♔h8
The starting move in the plan.
18 ♕e1 ♖g8
The second phase...
19 ♕f2 ♘ed7 20 ♘c2 ♗d8
Black is near to completing the
Fischer plan. Instead of the passive e7-square, Black will deploy
the bishop on the more aggressive c7-square, where it performs
a multitude of tasks: from c7, the
bishop defends the vulnerable
d6- and b6-squares but, more importantly, it eyes up the h2-pawn
as a possible target. Note that the
Fischer plan does not in any way
compromise Black's basic structure until it is favourable to do so.
It is important that Black is able
simply to rearrange his pieces

back to their original formation if necessary as White may yet play f3-f4.

21 ♕g3 ♘e5 22 ♘a3 ♕b8 23 ♕f2 ♘ed7 24 ♖c2 ♗c7 25 ♖cd2 *(D)*

White has made very little impression on Black's pawn structure whilst Black has carefully implemented the springboard to the Fischer attack. Therefore...

25...g5! *(D)*

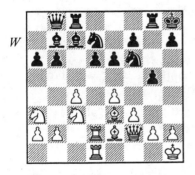

What does Black gain from such a huge concession to the protection around his king and his pawn structure?

Firstly, it is important to note that the attacking gesture ...g5 by itself is not justification enough. Indeed, the preparation of the attack, ...♔h8, ...♖g8, ...♗e7-d8-c7, is the reason why ...g5 is such a strong move. Black cannot and must not do without these moves. However, the onus is on White to distract his opponent by creating his own threats. If Black is allowed to set up the necessary minor-piece formation as above, then ...g5 and more importantly ...g5-g4 can have a devastating attack. As well as an attacking gesture at the white king, ...g5 is also an attempt to bring the bishop on b7 into the fray. One of the main ideas of the Polugaevsky system against the Hedgehog is to dampen the effect of Black's light-squared bishop on b7 by bolstering the e4-pawn. By playing ...g5, and eventually ...g4, Black is thematically trying to undermine White's pawn chain.

26 g4

Yet another thematic response as White counters with the standard idea against the Fischer attack – preventing the further advance of the g-pawn. Unfortunately, White's minor pieces are not in any position to aid his king and Black has a strong attack.

What if White were to play less thematically and allow the advance of the g-pawn?

a) 26 ♘c2 ♖g6 27 ♘d4 ♖cg8 28 ♗f1 g4! and White is without a constructive plan.

b) 26 ♗d4 ♘e5 27 ♗f1 ♖g6 28 g3 h5 29 ♗g2 ♔h7 30 b3 ♖cg8 and though White is obviously still in the game, Black's attack is promising.

A more successful g4 by White was seen in the game Popović-Polgar, Novi Sad 1990 which went 1 c4 c5 2 ♘f3 e6 3 d4 cxd4 4 ♘xd4 ♘c6 5 ♘b5 d6 6 c4 ♘f6 7 ♘1c3 a6 8 ♘a3 b6 9 ♗e2 ♗b7 10 0-0 ♘b8 11 f3 ♘bd7 12 ♗f4! ♕c7 13 ♕d2 ♗e7 14 ♖fd1 ♘e5 15 ♖ac1 0-0 16 ♗e3! ♘ed7?! 17 ♗f1 ♖ac8 18 ♕f2 ♗d8!? 19 ♖c2 ♕b8 20 ♖cd2 ♗c7 and before Black could execute the second phase of the Fischer Attack, White interjected with 21 g4!.

26...♘e5 27 ♗xb6?

A tactical miscalculation which simply works out in Black's favour. Better was 27 ♗d4 when Black still has to unravel to progress further with the attack.

27...♗xb6 28 ♕xb6 ♘exg4! 29 ♖xd6 *(D)* **♖c6!!**

And White can no longer defend both d6 and f2.

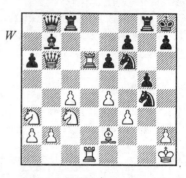

30 ♕d8

30 ♕d4 leads to the same conclusion after 30...♖xd6 31 ♕xd6 ♘f2+, while 30 ♖xc6?? allows 30...♕xh2 mate.

30...♖xd6 31 ♕xd6 ♘f2+ 32 ♔g1 ♘xd1 33 ♕xb8 ♖xb8 34 ♗xd1 ♘d7 35 ♔f2 ♔g7 36 ♘c2 ♘e5 37 ♗e2 ♖c8 38 ♘e3 a5 39 a3 ♗a6 40 b3 ♔f6 41 ♘b1 0-1

White resigned before Black could play 41...a4! with a simple win.

The previous game was a slightly one-sided view of a system which is extremely risky in practice. The next game is a more realistic picture of what can happen when White is fully aware of the consequences of the Fischer attack and does his best to frustrate Black's plans.

Game 2
Anand-Zso.Polgar
Delhi 1990

1 e4 c5 2 ♘f3 e6 3 d4 cxd4 4 ♘xd4 ♘c6 5 ♘b5 d6 6 c4 ♘f6 7 ♘1c3 a6 8 ♘a3 b6 9 ♗e2 ♗b7 10 0-0 ♘b8 11 f3 ♗e7 12 ♗e3 ♘bd7 13 ♕d2 0-0 14 ♖fd1 ♕c7 15 ♖ac1 ♖ac8 16 ♔h1 ♕b8 17 ♗f1 ♔h8 18 ♘c2 ♖g8?! *(D)*

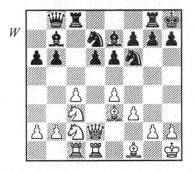

19 b3

We have reached, via a Taimanov move-order, a similar position to the previous game. However, there are some subtle differences which differentiate the two. The most noticeable difference is that White has decided to re-deploy the knight on a3 immediately to the more useful c2-square. White's most cunning ploy, however, has been to delay slightly the Polugaevsky formation by not playing his queen to f2 as early as in the previous

game. This has the effect of preventing one of the main components of the Fischer attack in that Black is prevented from playing ...♗e7-d8-c7 as her d-pawn is still attacked twice.

Black kicked off with 17...♔h8 but should have been more aware of White's idea and delayed committing her rook to g8 so quickly. It would have been better to revert to a more standard Hedgehog plan by playing 17...♖fe8 or 17...♘e5.

19...♗c6 20 ♗g1 *(D)*

White has cleverly prepared for the ...g5 thrust and it is still not too late to revert back to the standard formations, even at the cost of losing a move with 20...♖ge8. Although White has prepared for the Fischer attack, he has not however organised his pieces to counter the more standard Hedgehog plans of ...b5 and ...d5.

20...g5?!

20...b5? highlights one of the advantages of having the knight on c2 after 21 cxb5 axb5 22 ♘b4! when Black is helpless against ♘xc6 followed by ♘xb5.

21 ♖e1! ♖g6 22 ♘d5!

An extremely strong move which at first does not seem to threaten much but in fact gives White a clear advantage.

In general, Black will do well to realise that the Hedgehog pawn formation is held together by his minor pieces. Hence the more minor pieces are exchanged, the more Black's flimsy pawn structure is weakened. Here, in addition, Black has further accentuated the problem by playing the weakening ...g5.

22...♗d8 23 ♘xf6 ♘xf6 24 ♗d3

With the threat of 24 e5 attacking the rook on g6.

24...♘h5 25 ♗d4+

25 e5 ♖h6! ∓.

25...e5

Anand points out 25...♔g8 26 ♘e3 ♘f4 27 ♗b1 with a clear advantage to White.

26 ♗e3

If 26 ♗b2, then 26...g4 (26...♘f4 27 ♘e3 with a clear advantage to White) 27 f4 (27 fxg4 ♖xg4 28 ♕h6 ♘f4) 27...♔g8 28 f5 ♗g5 29 ♘e3 and

though White has a slight advantage, the game continuation is better.

26...g4 27 fxg4 ♘f6 (D)

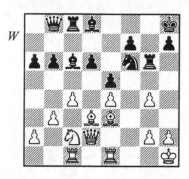

28 ♘b4!

And suddenly all of Black's previous weakening moves catch up with her. Black can now never recover.

28...♗xe4 29 h3 ♕b7 30 ♘d5! ♗xd3 31 ♕xd3 b5 32 ♘xf6 ♖xf6 33 ♕d5 ♕d7 34 cxb5 ♖xc1 35 ♖xc1 axb5 36 ♕a8 ♖g6 37 ♗b6 ♖g8 38 ♖c8 ♕xc8 39 ♕xc8 ♗xb6 40 ♕c6 ♗c5 41 ♕xb5 e4 42 b4 ♗f2 43 ♕e2 e3 44 ♕b2+! ♖g7 45 b5 d5 46 b6± ♗g3 47 b7 f6 48 b8♕+ ♗xb8 49 ♕xb8+ ♖g8 50 ♕a7 1-0

A flawless and simple victory for White. It is clear that Black must not religiously play the Fischer attack against any formation White may adopt, but should feign the attack instead of actually carrying it out.

Doing nothing!

In the last ten pages, I have shown thematic ways by which Black can seek activity in the Hedgehog. The best policy in the Hedgehog, however, is simply to do nothing and wait for White. I realise that this may not be sufficient if Black needs to play for a win, but then Black can adopt some of the other plans outlined previously.

In normal tournament circumstances, White has the first move advantage and therefore Black should patiently wait for his chance. The Hedgehog gives Black the opportunity to frustrate White and then strike at just the right moment. Who better than Karpov to show us the merits of doing nothing:

Game 3
Jadoul-Karpov
Brussels 1986

1 e4 c5 2 ᐃf3 e6 3 d4 cxd4 4 ᐃxd4 ᐃc6 5 ᐃb5 d6 6 c4 ᐃf6 7 ᐃ1c3 a6 8 ᐃa3 ᐵe7 9 ᐵe2 0-0 10 0-0 b6 11 ᐵe3 ᐵb7 12 ♕b3 ᐃd7 13 ᔐfd1 ᐃc5 *(D)* 14 ♕c2

This is the main line of the Sicilian Taimanov and yet it took me a long time to work out 14 ᐵxc5 bxc5 15 ♕xb7? ᐃa5! – winning the queen!

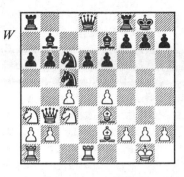

14...♕c7 15 ᔐac1 ᔐac8 16 ᐃab1!?

One of the main reasons for Black reverting to this system is the awkward positioning of this knight, which is completely out of the game on a3. Here, White attempts to re-route this knight to the more active d2-square but at the cost of giving Black time to reorganise as well. On d2, moreover, the knight hinders the d1-rook's influence on the d5-square.

16...ᐃe5 17 ᐃd2 ᐃcd7 18 a3 ᔐfe8 19 b4 ᐃf6 20 h3 *(D)*

20...ᐃg6

A move designed to discourage White from playing f4.

21 ♕b1 ♗a8 22 ♘a4 ♖b8 23 ♗f1 h6 24 g3 ♘d7 25 ♗g2 ♖bc8

A typical Hedgehog struggle. White has no clear plan and is simply shuffling his pieces to different squares in the hope that Black will allow a tactic. Meanwhile, Black is poised to take advantage of any slightly ambitious plan that White may conjure up.

26 ♘b3 *(D)*

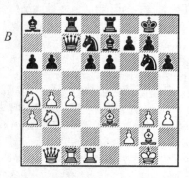

26...♕b7!

This move is not directed at an attack on the e4-pawn but merely a 'constructive' move which keeps White guessing. Of course Black will not play ...f5 though White may be wondering about a plan consisting of ...♖f8, ...f5-f4.

27 ♕a2 ♕b8

The queen simply returns to b8.

28 c5?!

White's patience finally snaps and he somewhat clumsily lunges forward on the queenside. Note how Black's pieces are perfectly placed for the ensuing counter-attack: the bishop is on a8 thereby preventing White from gaining a tempo with ♘a5 and c5-c6 and the knight is on g6 where it aids the cause of ...h5-h4.

28...b5 29 ♘b2 ♘f6 30 ♕b1 *(D)*

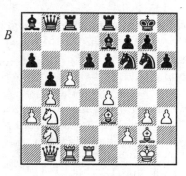

30...h5! 31 ♘a5?!

The better alternative was 31 cxd6 ♗xd6 32 ♘c5 ♗xc5! 33 bxc5 h4! but White has no way of holding on to the two bishops after 34 g4 ♘f4! 35 ♗xf4 (35 f3? ♘xg2 36 ♔xg2 ♕g3+) 35...♕xf4 and Black is fine.

31...dxc5 32 bxc5 h4! 33 g4 ♘f4∓ 34 ♗xf4 ♕xf4 35 ♘d3 ♕c7 36 ♕b4 ♘xe4! 37 ♗xe4 ♗xe4 38 ♕xe4 ♕xa5 39 c6 ♗xa3 40 ♖a1 ♕c3 41 ♘e5 ♗b2 0-1

The perfect illustration.

Miscellaneous ideas

We have now covered the majority of Black's possible counter-attacking ideas in the Hedgehog. Occasionally, Black develops some new possibilities but these are rarely seen again as they are probably too ambitious and therefore unsound! Nevertheless, for the sake of completeness if nothing else, I shall outline some of the more unusual ideas that I have found.

The ...f5!? idea

After 1...♗e5 2 ♗f1, Yudasin-Rublevsky, USSR Ch 1991 went 2...f5!?. Black again strikes at the heart of the Maroczy Bind but this time on the kingside rather than on the queenside with the customary ...b5. Play then continued 3 exf5 ♖xf5 4 ♘e2 ♕f6 and Black developed with tempo and won in 37 moves.

The above example certainly worked well for Black but I would say that White's pieces were badly placed and in general, the ...f5 idea can be dealt with quite easily in most circumstances:

In the above position, Black again ambitiously played 1...f5?! to which White replied 2 ♘b4! f4 3 ♘xc6 ♕xc6 4 ♕d2 ♘e5 5 b4! ♕c7 6 ♘a4 a5 7 bxa5 bxa5 8 c5! and Black never had enough time to organise anything on the kingside and had thus given up a bishop for no compensation.

Black advances ...h7-h5-h4

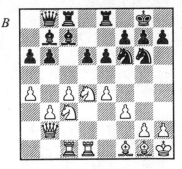

Here Black has implemented the first stage of the Fischer plan (...♗e7-d8-c7) but his knight on g6 hinders the g7-pawn. Instead, the game Chandler-Wolff, London 1990 went 1...h5!? 2 b4 h4 3 ♖e1 ♘h5 and White played the dubious 4 ♕d2 when after 4...d5!, due to the threat of ...♗f4, White had to return to a2 with the queen and the players soon agreed a draw. However, Black already had a slight advantage.

Black plays ...e6-e5!?

This is the most surprising and perhaps the best of the off-beat ideas I have seen. Yudasin-Lautier, Pamplona 1992/3 continued 1...e5!?, which seemingly gives up all protection of the vital d5-square. A closer examination, however, shows that Black also has a massive grip on d4. White played 2 ♘d5 ♘e6! 3 ♕e3 ♘cd4 4 ♖cd2 ♗xd5!? 5 cxd5 ♘c5 6 b4 ♘a4 7 ♗xa6 ♖c7 8 ♗f1 b5! when Black had clear compensation for the pawn and in fact went on to win the game.

The reader should note that though the possibility of ...e5 exists with the dark-squared bishops still on the board, Black would then have a bad bishop compared to White's counterpart which adds protection to the d4-square.

2 Scheveningen systems

Although White can force Black into a Hedgehog formation in the Sicilian Kan, many players either do not like the slow manoeuvring in these systems or they prefer the more traditional set-ups for White against the Sicilian.

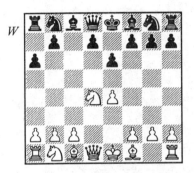

The above position is the earliest moment that White can introduce 5 ♘c3, blocking in the c-pawn and introducing a host of new ideas and problems for Black to solve. So what are these new ideas for White and the antidotes for Black?

A typical line in this variation might continue 5...♕c7 (not 5...♘f6? as 6 e5! is now possible!) 6 ♗d3 ♘f6 7 0-0 d6 8 ♔h1 ♗e7 9 f4 − White does not hide his intentions of a kingside attack and Black seemingly passively huddles behind his pawn shelter hoping for counterplay on the queenside. However, White's present pawn structure has some weaknesses (as well as strengths) that Black can take advantage of:

Black plays ...e5

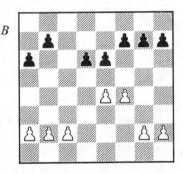

If we take the basic pawn structure of the position and assume that it is Black to move, after 1...e5! we can safely say that Black has a slight structural advantage. This sweeping statement can be corroborated after 2 fxe5 dxe5, when we have a new pawn structure which greatly favours Black:

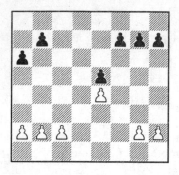

Now, we notice that White has an isolated pawn and in addition Black has only two pawn islands compared to White's three. In fact, whatever White does, he cannot get away from a worse pawn structure. Even if he does not exchange on e5 and maintains the tension in the centre, Black can still claim a positional advantage with the following position:

Black has exchanged on f4 and though he has a weak pawn on d6, White has a similar counterpart on e4. More importantly, the pawn exchange on f4 has meant that Black can claim the e5-square as his own as no white pawns can ever cover this square. Additionally, Black always retains the option of getting rid of his d6-pawn by playing ...d5! at an opportune moment whereas White has no such option as the e4-pawn is firmly blockaded.

The last option that White has at his disposal is to pass up the chance of exchanging pawns and push the f-pawn to f5.

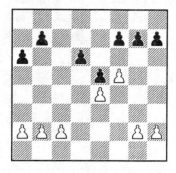

Although this option is the least of the evils mentioned so far, White still cannot get away from his weak e-pawn. However, it is true that Black also has a weakness on d6 as well as d5 and thus this option may seem to give White the advantage. The key, however, lies in who has more protection over d5. This is why looking at basic pawn formations is not enough to assess a position and more complex positions are needed to prove the point:

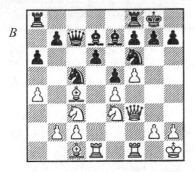

In the above diagram, Black had played ...e5 to which White had answered f5. Black, however, is at a serious disadvantage as he has not overprotected the d5-square. It is essential that if the ...e5 idea is to be correctly executed, Black must assess the position resulting after f5 by White and his chances of playing the liberating ...d5 break.

A more viable ...e5 can be seen here: after 1...e5! 2 f5 Black has more than adequate cover of d5 and can claim the advantage after 2...d5!.

An example of further complications can be seen in the next diagram:

Here, with Black to move, 1...e5? is a serious mistake as White can play 2 ♘f5! with a very dangerous, if not winning attack. The reader might well think 'how Black can stop such a manoeuvre and hence ever play the ...e5 break?'. The answer lies in nuances in the opening. After 1 e4 c5 2 ♘f3 e6 3 d4 cxd4 4 ♘xd4 a6 5 ♘c3 ♕c7 6 ♗d3 ♘f6 7 0-0, one of Black's main moves is 7...♗c5!? when Black loses a tempo after 8 ♘b3 ♗e7 but he manages to divert the white knight on d4 to the less active square b3. Hence now, the ...e5 break is perfectly safe and after some 'normal' developing moves, Black should seek to play this as soon as possible. The idea to dislodge the knight from d4 is a major theme in the Sicilian, particularly those with a Scheveningen nature. In the real Scheveningen, Black challenges the knight on d4 by playing ...♘c6 and other offsprings of this idea have started to crop up in the shape of 1 e4 c5 2 ♘f3 ♘c6 3 d4 cxd4 4 ♘xd4 ♕b6!? and after 5 ♘b3, the black queen usually returns to c7, its natural square, after she has managed to divert the knight from d4 to b3. This idea is also possible in the Kan (the above example is a Taimanov move order) after 1 e4 c5 2 ♘f3 e6 3 d4 cxd4 4 ♘xd4 a6 5 ♗d3 ♕b6 though 6 c3! instead of 6 ♘b3?! is known to give White an advantage. Black also has to watch out for White's e5 ideas. One interesting method to prevent this advance (instead of simply protecting the e5-square) can be seen in the following diagram:

Here, with Black to move, the game Emms-I.Gurevich, Hastings Challengers 1991 went 1...♖ad8! 2 e5?! dxe5 3 fxe5 ♕xe5!! - the rook on d8 indirectly attacks the d4-knight. Of course White did not have to fall into the trap, but then Black would simply build up towards his own ...e5 break by playing ...♖fe8, ...♗f8, ...g6 (protecting the f5-square), ...♗g7 and finally ...e5. Note that if White moves his knight from the indirect attack of the rook on d8 via ♘f3, Black would immediately reply ...e5! with a good game.

Black plays ...d5

Occasionally, Black can play the ...d5 break without the inclusion of ...e5:

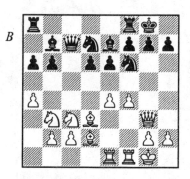

In the above position, Black, in Howell-Emms, Cappelle la Grande 1994, played 1...d5! and after 2 exd5 ♘xd5 3 ♘xd5 ♗xd5 4 ♕h3 f5!, Black had a small advantage. If White had played 2 e5?! instead of 2 exd5, Black would have countered with 2...♘e4! and after 3 ♘xe4 dxe4 4 ♗xe4 ♗xe4 5 ♖xe4 ♕xc2, Black is again better.

The above example is rare and Black usually plays ...d5 in one stroke when White has castled queenside and expanded on the kingside with g4:

After the moves 1 e4 c5 2 ♘f3 e6 3 d4 cxd4 4 ♘xd4 a6 5 ♘c3 ♕c7 6 f4 b5 7 ♗d3 ♗b7 8 ♕f3 ♘f6 9 ♗e3 ♘c6 10 0-0-0 in Tolnai-Polgar, Hungarian Ch 1994 Black played 10...b4 11 ♘ce2 ♘a5 and after 12 g4 d5! 13 e5 ♘d7 14 ♔b1 ♘c4 15 ♗c1 0-0-0 16 h4 ♘c5, Black had a good game and won in 48 moves.

The following annotated game is not of theoretical importance to the precise lines we are discuss-

ing as the opening is actually the Boleslavsky Variation of the Sicilian Defence, a system with a different set of ideas and nuances from the Kan. However, the game incorporates what all Sicilian players should be striving for (primarily what has been shown by example with the ...e5 and ...d5 breaks in this chapter), and is one of the 'cleanest' and most clear-cut Sicilian wins I have seen to date:

Game 4
Unzicker-Taimanov
Stockholm IZ 1952

1 e4 c5 2 ♘f3 ♘c6 3 d4 cxd4 4 ♘xd4 ♘f6 5 ♘c3 d6 6 ♗e2 *(D)*

6 ...   e5

Of course, in the Kan, we do not have the luxury of playing this move in one go as our e-pawn is committed to e6 on move 2. Nevertheless, the reader should not think of this as a disadvantage as holding back with ...e5 can often pose White greater problems. It is true that via this system (and the Najdorf) Black seemingly saves a move, but he pays a price for this in the shape of the weakness on d5. Many players, Kasparov included, prefer to delay ...e5 until it is favourable for Black to play it. In fact Kasparov, when faced with 1 e4 c5 2 ♘f3 d6 3 d4 cxd4 4 ♘xd4 ♘f6 5 ♘c3 a6 6 ♗e2 refrains from playing the recommended 6...e5 and favours the Scheveningen (and the Kan) approach of playing 6...e6.

7 ♘f3   h6

A necessary precaution now that Black has committed himself with ...e5. Without this move, White would happily trade his dark-squared bishop via ♗g5xf6 for one of Black's main defenders of the d5-square.

8 0-0   ♗e7
9 ♖e1

Taimanov describes this as a move which hinders ...d5 due to the 'x-ray' on the e5-pawn by the rook on e1.

9 ...   0-0
10 h3?   a6
11 ♗f1   b5
12 a3?

A weak move which gives Black a free hand. More active and clearly superior is **12 a4 b4 13 ♘d5 ♘xd5 14 exd5 ♘a5 15 ♗d2 ♖b8** with unclear play.

12 ...   ♗b7
13 b3   ♖c8
14 ♗b2 *(D)*

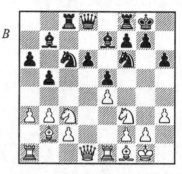

14 ...   ♖c7!

An excellent move. Black prepares for doubling the rooks on the semi-open c-file and at the same time the queen is given the opportunity of further overprotecting d5 and attacking White's e4-pawn by going to a8.

15 ♘b1   ♕a8
16 ♘bd2 *(D)*

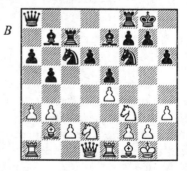

| 16 | ... | ♘d8! |

16...♖fc8 would have 'fallen' for White's idea of 17 c4!. Black cleverly gives White more to think about than the freeing manoeuvre ...d5. c4 can still be played by White but at the cost of fatally weakening d4, of which the black knight on d8 is ready to take advantage with ...♘d8-e6.

| 17 | ♗d3 | ♘e6 |
| 18 | ♖c1 | ♖fc8 |

The first stage of Black's plan is fully implemented. Through ingenious manoeuvring, Black has more protection of d5 than White (through his policy of overprotection) and he has full use of the semi-open c-file for his rooks.

The hardest part of the game, however, is still to be played out. Notice that Black 'teases' White with the threat of ...d5 for as long as possible. A perfect example of the threat being better than the execution.

19	♘h2	♘d7
20	♘hf1	♘dc5
21	♘g3	g6
22	♘e2!	

A cunning trap. In *Winning with the Sicilian*, Taimanov gives the variation 22...♘xe4? 23 ♘xe4 ♗xe4 24 ♗xe4 ♕xe4 25 ♘c3! and at the cost of a mere pawn, White has bought himself

out of a serious disadvantage and may even have the upper hand. However...

| 22 | ... | ♗g5! |

The final piece of the jigsaw as even the traditionally bad bishop on e7 finds a good diagonal and even aids the cause of ...d5.

| 23 | ♘c3 | ♘d4 |
| 24 | ♘cb1 *(D)* | |

B

| 24 | ... | d5! |

Finally White is put out of his misery and Black smashes open the position.

| 25 | exd5 | |

25 ♗xd4? fails to 25...♘xd3.

25	...	♘xd3
26	cxd3	♖xc1
27	♗xc1	♗xd5
28	f3	♖c2
29	a4	b4
30	♔h1	♕c6

And in this position, with no direct threats, White resigned! In the next few moves Black will simply play ...♗f4 and ...♘f5-g3 with devastating consequences.

0-1

Queenside expansion with ...b5

Black's fourth move, 4...a6, is mainly used to prevent White from attacking the black queen on c7 with ♘b5. However, it is also the springboard to the standard Sicilian queenside expansion involving ...b5. It should be noted that although the further advance of this pawn might enable Black to launch some sort of minority attack in the future, the main purpose of ...b5 in the Kan is to re-deploy the light-squared bishop to b7 where it can pressurise White's e4-pawn and control the vital d5-square. Hence, it is also a viable option for Black to occasionally play ...b6 instead of ...b5.

Nevertheless, if Black does choose to expand on the queenside with ...b5, he must be careful of certain tricks that White has at its disposal. At best (and it is the usual response from the majority White players), White will let Black 'get away' with ...b5 by simply playing ...a3, taking the precaution of not allowing Black to play ...b4 which

would further strengthen his grip on d5.

One of the most important points to consider for Black players is not to play ...b5 too early:

The game Martin-Mortazavi, British Ch 1992 began 1 ♘f3 c5 2 e4 e6 3 d4 cxd4 4 ♘xd4 a6 5 ♘c3 ♕c7 6 ♗e2 b5?! 7 0-0 ♗b7 8 ♗f3! d6 *(D)* (8...♘f6? 9 e5!).

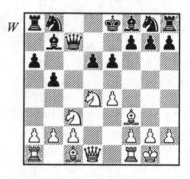

Black has played ...b5 far too early and White took immediate advantage of this with 9 a4! b4 10 ♘a2! ♘f6 and instead of 11 ♘xb4, which would give Black a good game after 11...d5!, White continued 11 ♖e1! and I was forced to weaken the b5-square by supporting my b-pawn with ...a5. The game continued 11...♗e7 12 ♗d2! a5 13 c3 bxc3 14 ♘xc3 0-0 15 ♘db5 ♕d7 16 ♗f4 ♖d8 17 ♖c1 ♘c6?! (17 ...♘a6 is better) 18 ♘d5! ±. Consider this *(D)*:

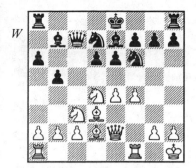

Here again, Black has committed himself too early and though White can claim an advantage after 12 a4!, with the same idea as the Martin-Mortazavi example, Short-Seirawan, Amsterdam 1983, saw a different plan with 12 b4!, a move which believe it or not is directed at the a6-pawn!. The game continued 12...0-0 13 a4 bxa4 14 ♖xa4 ♘b6 15 ♖aa1 g6 16 ♗xa6 ♖xa6 17 ♖xa6 e5 18 ♘b3 ♗xa6 19 ♕xa6 exf4 20 ♖xf4 ♖c8 21 ♕f1!, and again the position is ±.

White plays g4-g5

This used to be a very popular plan in the 1970s though since the famous Karpov-Kasparov game in their World Championship contest in Moscow, White players have switched to other systems as Kasparov showed Black's many resources. From a theoretical point of view, the next

game is of no real interest to the Kan player, though from an 'ideas' angle, it is an essential guide:

Game 5
Karpov-Kasparov
Moscow Wch (24) 1985

1 e4 c5 2 ♘f3 d6 3 d4 cxd4 4 ♘xd4 ♘f6 5 ♘c3 a6 6 ♗e2 e6

Nowadays, most Najdorf players would play 6...e5. However Kasparov has long been a fan of the Scheveningen Sicilian and often transposes to this variation via a Najdorf in order to avoid the dreaded Keres Attack against the Scheveningen.

7	0-0	♗e7
8	f4	0-0
9	♔h1	♕c7 *(D)*

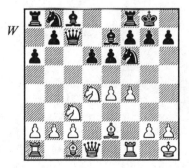

We can also reach this position via a Kan move order (1 e4 c5 2 ♘f3 e6 3 d4 cxd4 4 ♘xd4 a6 5 ♘c3 ♕c7 6 ♗e2 ♘f6 7 0-0 d6 8

f4 ♗e7 9 ♔h1 0-0), which is why I have chosen to annotate this game.

10 a4

Karpov-Kasparov, Moscow Wch (5) 1984/5 went **10 ♗f3** ♘c6 11 a4 ♖e8 12 ♗e3 ♖b8 13 ♖e1 ♗d7 14 ♕d3 ♘xd4 15 ♗xd4 e5! 16 ♗a7 ♖bc8 17 ♗e3 ♕c4 18 a5 h6 19 h3 ♗f8 20 ♗d2 ♕d4 21 ♗e3 ♕b4 with a draw by repetition.

10 ...   ♘c6
11 ♗e3   ♖e8 *(D)*

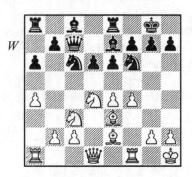

12 ♗f3

Geller's recommended plan of **12 ♗g1** was seen in Karpov-Kasparov, Moscow Wch (10) 1985 when Kasparov improved over Geller-Polugaevsky, USSR Ch 1983 with 12...♖b8! (the Geller game went 12...e5?! 13 ♘b3 exf4 14 a5! ♘e5 15 ♖xf4 ♗e6 16 ♘d5 ±) 13 ♕d2 e5 14 ♘b3 ♘a5 15 ♘xa5 ♕xa5 16 ♗a7 ♖a8 17

♗e3 ♕b4!?. Kasparov later claimed that 17...exf4 and then 18 ♗xf4 ♗e6 or 18 ♖xf4 ♗e6 19 ♗d4 ♘d7 was equal, though Schiller and Shamkovich in *Kasparov's Opening Repertoire* say that White has an advantage after 18 ♗xf4 ♗e6 19 ♘d5 ♕xd2 20 ♘xe7+ ♖xe7 21 ♗xd2.

Another example of the g4 plan was seen in Tal-Kasparov, Brussels SWIFT Blitz 1987 when White played **12 g4** and after 12...♘xd4 13 ♕xd4 ♘d7 (13...e5! =) 14 g5 b6 15 ♗f3 ♗b7 16 ♗g2 ♗f8 17 ♕d2 ♖ac8 18 f5 ♕c4 19 g6 hxg6 20 fxg6 fxg6 21 ♕f2 ♘f6 22 ♕g3 e5 and the game was agreed a draw.

12 ...   ♖b8

A necessary move now that White has posted his light squared bishop on f3. 12...♖b8 side-steps any tricks on the a8-h1 diagonal and also lends support to a future ...b5.

13 ♕d2   ♗d7
14 ♘b3!?

Applauded by Schiller and Shamkovich, though there are some drawbacks to this move. 14 ♘b3 avoids the exchange of knights in the centre followed by the thematic ...e5 by Black which we know as an equalising move but it has the disadvantage of removing a minor piece from the scene of the action on the king-side.

In game 2 of the match, Karpov played **14 ♕f2** and there followed 14...♘xd4 15 ♗xd4 e5 16 ♗e3 ♗e6?!.

14 ... b6 *(D)*

15 g4!?

After many lacklustre attempts at probing the black position, Karpov finally chooses the most aggressive continuation. The reader should note, however, that g4 is not merely an attacking gesture on White's part. White often plays this way in order merely to gain more freedom and space for his minor pieces and can just as well concentrate on Black's weakness on d6 as well his king.

15 ... ♗c8
16 g5 ♘d7
17 ♕f2!

A necessary precaution as after 17 ♗g2?, Black would shut out

the rook on a1 with 17...♘a5! 18 ♕f2 ♘c4 19 ♗c1.

17 ... ♗f8

Now if **17...♘a5**, 18 ♖ad1 and the white bishop will happily retreat to c1.

18 ♗g2 ♗b7
19 ♖ad1 g6

The best defence against White's formation. With the dark-squared bishop on g7, Black's chances of getting mated are considerably reduced.

20 ♗c1 ♖bc8
21 ♖d3! ♘b4
22 ♖h3 ♗g7
23 ♗e3 *(D)*

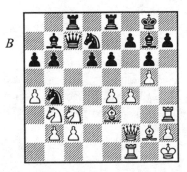

23 ... ♖e7!

A brilliant concept, which has now become a standard plan for Sicilian players facing such a pawn-storm. Black doubles rooks on the e-file in preparation for his 25th move, which gives White the option of opening this file.

24 &g1

24 ♕h4 h5! 25 gxh6 followed by the blockade of the h-pawn by the black king is a well-known defensive resource in the Sicilian.

24	...	♖ce8
25	♖d1	f5!
26	gxf6	

If White had played **26 exf5**, then after 26...exf5 Black's forces are in their optimum position to begin a counterattack. Notice how d5 is adequately covered by the knight on b4 and the bishop on b7 and the rooks on the e-file guarantee Black a good game.

26	...	♘xf6
27	♖g3	♖f7
28	♗xb6	♕b8
29	♗e3	♘h5
30	♖g4	

30 ♖f3? would be met with 30...♗xc3! 31 bxc3 ♘a2! ∓.

| 30 | ... | ♘f6 |
| 31 | ♖h4 *(D)* | |

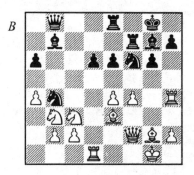

34 ... g5

Karpov was forced to play 31 ♖h4 in order to have any chance of retaining his title, but this move simply fails to Kasparov's reply.

32 fxg5 ♘g4! 33 ♕d2 ♘xe3 34 ♕xe3 ♘xc2 35 ♕b6 ♗a8! ∓ 36 ♖xd6 ♖b7 37 ♕xa6 ♖xb3 38 ♖xe6 ♖xb2 39 ♕c4 &h8 40 e5 ♕a7+ 41 &h1 ♗xg2+ 42 &xg2 ♘d4+ 0-1

An impressive victory by Black though one striking factor was that Kasparov timed his counterplay and defensive formation to perfection. Indeed, timing is one of the hardest concepts in the Sicilian and often, though a player may know all the best defensive and counterattacking possibilities, he may leave it too late:

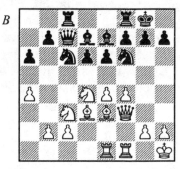

Here, in Hennigan-Hamid, British Ch 1994, Black made one inaccuracy too many and played 13...♘b4? to which White countered 14 g4! placing Black in a very difficult position. White converted the win very quickly after 14...♘e8 15 g5 f6 16 ♕h3 e5 17 ♘e6 ♕c6 18 f5 ♗xe6 19 fxe6 ♘c7 20 ♖g1 fxg5 21 ♗xg5 ♘xd3 22 cxd3 ♗xg5 23 ♖xg5 ♖ce8 24 ♖h5 ♘xe6 25 ♖xh7 ♘f4 26 ♖g1 ♕c7 27 ♖h8+ ♔f7 28 ♕f5+ ♔e7 29 ♖xg7+ ♔d8 30 ♖xc7 1-0.

The writing was on the wall when after 14 g4!, Black had no option but to retreat her knight to e8, hardly an active plan against g4. From the Kasparov game, we should note the importance of the rook on f8 and the knight on c6. It is clear that Black should play the move ...♖fe8 in order to maintain the option of ...♗f8, ...g6 and ♗g7 as in the Kasparov game. In addition, any knight ventures from c6 should be first seriously thought out as one of Black's main ideas against g4 is to play ...♘xd4 and ...e5. Notice that Kasparov only played ...♘b4 when Karpov had retreated his knight from d4 to b3, thereby removing the possibility of the ...♘xd4 and ...e5 idea.

Another common mistake by Black can be seen from the following diagram:

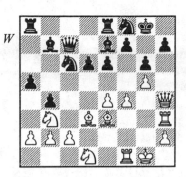

Again, Black has left it too late (his bishop should be on g7) and his knight on f8 cannot possibly defend against White's entire army. 20 f5! exf5 21 exf5 ♘e5 22 ♘d4 ♗d8 23 f6 h5 24 ♗e2 ♕d7 25 ♖f4! and White comes bursting through on the kingside.

Occasionally, White gets it all wrong and is tempted by the g4 thrust before Black has even castled:

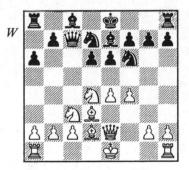

In the above diagram, White in Izumikawa-Mortazavi, San Francisco 1994 tried to dissuade

Black from castling kingside by 10 g4!?. However, as Black has maintained maximum flexibility with his king position and his queenside pawns, he grabbed the initiative with 10...♘c5 11 g5 ♘fd7 12 ♗c4?! (far better would have been 12 b4! with an advantage to White; see next section) b5 13 ♗d5 ♗b7! 14 ♗xb7 ♕xb7 15 b4 ♘a4! 16 ♘xa4 bxa4 17 ♖b1? ♘c5! ∓.

Thus from the examples given, we can see that g4 by White can be a dangerous and potent move but if Black can time his defensive manoeuvres well, he is not without counterplay.

The bishop on d3

One of the trademarks of the white set-up against the Kan is that of the aggressively placed light-squared bishop on d3. In other Sicilians, this bishop is rarely allowed to this aggressive post and must either take refuge on e2 or boldly go to c4 as in the Sozin and Velimirović attacks. In *Winning with the Sicilian*, Taimanov describes the bishop on d3 as 'in the zone of the black knights', meaning that Black can often 'attack' this bishop with ...♘c6-e5, ...♘d7-e5 or in some

cases ...♘c6-b4. Superficially, this may seem like a good plan as Black would then net the two bishops and remove one of White's main attacking pieces, aimed at the black kingside. However, as usual, there are certain exceptions to the rule, where White would gladly give up the two bishops for a positional advantage.

One of the exceptions to the rule has already been seen in this chapter in the game Hennigan-Hamid when Black went falsely in search of the two bishops only to be swiftly mated on the kingside by White's other pieces. A better example can be seen in the following diagram:

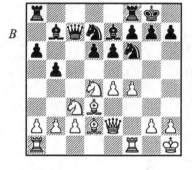

Here, Black tried to grab the two bishops with 1...♘c5?! to which White answered 2 b4! and after 2...♘xd3 3 cxd3 (D) we have a new pawn structure and a completely different plan for White:

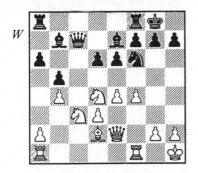

It is true that Black has gained the two bishops, normally a good thing, but at what price?

Firstly, White has 'repaired' his pawn structure and now lends support to the previously weak e4-pawn. This has the obvious side-effect of seriously lessening the influence of the bishop on b7 (it is now 'biting on granite') but the less obvious benefit is giving Black a bad pawn structure!

White can now use the weak a5-square for his knight with ♘d4-b3-a5 and the semi-open c-file for his rooks. In addition, the change in pawn structure has also deprived the black knight of the c4-square.

Perhaps the most important consequence of this dubious minor-piece exchange is that Black has lost much of this potency of his ...e5 idea. The reader will notice that after this thematic move, the e4-pawn is no longer a weakness in White's camp (see beginning of chapter) as White is firmly supporting it with the pawn on d3. Of course, ...d5 is completely out of the question as after e5, White has a very good version of the French Defence.

In principle, however, the two bishops *are* important and Black should merely be aware of exceptions to the rule.

3 Sicilian Kan – Main Line

If White so wishes, he can force Black into a Hedgehog formation. The simplest way of achieving this (dealt with in the next chapter) is by the following move-order:

1 e4 c5 2 ◊f3 e6 3 d4 cxd4 4 ◊xd4 a6 *(D)*

5 c4
However, this has the slight drawback of allowing Black to develop his pieces with maximum flexibility; for example, in this line Black is rarely forced to play an early ...d6. Instead, White now plays c4 at a later date with the following move-order:

1 e4 c5 2 ◊f3 e6 3 d4 cxd4 4 ◊xd4 a6 5 ◊d3 *(D)*

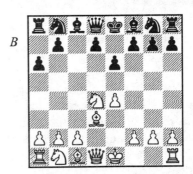

5 ...   ◊f6
5...◊c5 is now a major alternative, and is dealt with in annotated games 6 and 7.

Equally popular is **5...♕c7** and then ...◊f6.

There are other ideas:

a) Some players have delayed 5...◊f6 and played **5...♕c7** with the plan **6 0-0 ◊c5!?** (Brunner-Van Wely, Munich 1991 went 6...g6 7 c4 ◊g7 8 ◊e3 ◊f6 9 ◊c3 0-0 10 ♖c1 d6 11 f3 b6 12 ♕d2 ◊b7 13 ♖fd1 ◊bd7 14 ◊f1 ♖fd8 15 b4 ♖ac8 16 ◊b3 ◊f8 17 ♕f2 ◊a8 18 ♔h1 ♕b8 19 c5!? bxc5 20 bxc5 dxc5 21 ◊xa6 ◊b7 22 ◊b5 c4! 23 ◊a5 ◊e5! with the idea of ...◊d3 – compare 'b') **7 ◊b3 ◊e7 8 ♕g4 ◊f6** in mind:

a1) One antidote was introduced by ex-World Champion

Vassily Smyslov in Smyslov-I.Gurevich, Biel IZ 1993: **9 f4** d6 10 ♘c3 h5 11 ♕e2 ♘c6 12 ♗e3 ♗xc3 13 bxc3 ♘f6 14 h3 e5 15 ♕f2 exf4 16 ♗xf4 ♘e5 17 ♕g3 ♔f8 18 ♗g5 ♘h7 19 ♗d2 ♗d7 20 ♘d4 ♘f6 21 ♕h4 ♘g6 22 ♕f2 ♘e5 23 a4 ♖e8 24 a5 with a big advantage to White.

a2) Sicilian expert John Nunn tried a different approach against Gurevich but found himself in a slightly inferior position after **9** ♘**c3** h5 10 ♕e2 ♘c6 11 f4 d6 12 ♗e3?! ♗xc3! 13 bxc3 ♘f6 14 ♔h1 ♘g4 15 ♗g1 e5 16 f5 ♘b8! Nunn-I.Gurevich, Hastings 1992. A similar knight retreat can be seen in the game Ehlvest-Kasparov in the next chapter.

b) **5...g6!?** is another reasonable alternative which has been used on occasions by Grandmasters Lobron, Torre, Andersson, Van Wely, etc. The idea is to cut out all the Scheveningen lines and at the same time gain a favourable Hedgehog to the main line with possible deployment of the king's knight to e7 instead of f6. Examples of this include:

b1) **6 c4** ♗g7 and now:

b11) **7** ♘**e2** ♘f6 8 ♘bc3 0-0 9 0-0 d6 10 b3 ♘bd7 11 a4 b6 12 ♗a3 ♕c7 13 ♖c1 ♗b7 14 ♗b1 ♘c5 15 ♘g3 ♖ad8 16 b4 ♘cd7 17 ♕e2 ♖c8 18 ♗a2 ♘e5 and

Black is fine; Matthias-Hoffmann, Ippstadt 1993.

b12) **7** ♘**b3** ♘e7 8 ♘c3 0-0 9 0-0 ♘bc6 10 ♗g5 b6 11 ♕d2 d6 12 ♗e2 ♕d7 13 ♗h6 ♖d8 14 ♗xg7 ♔xg7 15 ♖ad1 ♕c7 16 f4 ♖b8 17 ♔h1 f6 18 ♖f3! with the idea of ♖d3 with a big advantage to White; Howell-Anand, Gausdal jr Wch 1986.

b2) Traditional Scheveningen-style mating ideas are somewhat stymied by the bishop being on g7 instead of e7. McDonald-Sadler, Dublin Telecom 1991 went **6 0-0** ♗g7 7 c3 d6 8 f4 ♘f6 9 ♘f3 0-0 10 ♕e1 ♘bd7 11 ♘bd2 b5 12 e5?! dxe5 13 fxe5 ♘g4 14 ♕e4 ♘gxe5 15 ♕xa8 ♕b6+ 16 ♔h1 ♗b7 17 ♕xf8+ ♗xf8 when Black's queen is stronger than the two rooks in the middlegame.

c) **5...**♘**c6!?** is also a viable option, though the resulting positions give Black very few winning chances. After **6** ♘**xc6** examples of this rarely seen possibility include:

c1) **6...dxc6** is the normal way to recapture:

c11) **7** ♘**d2** e5 8 a4 ♗d6 9 0-0 ♘e7 10 ♘c4 ♗c7 11 a5 ♘g6 12 ♗e3 ♗e6 13 ♕e1 ♘f4 14 ♕b4 ♘xd3 15 cxd3 ♕xd3 16 ♕xb7 0-0 17 ♕xc7 ♗xc4 18 ♕xe5 ♖fe8 19 ♕c5 ♖xe4 20 ♖fd1 ♕b3

21 ♕xc6 ♖ee8 22 ♖d2 and White had a clear advantage in Nijboer-Miles, Debrecen Echt 1992.

c12) **7 0-0 e5 8 a4 ♘f6 9 ♘d2** and then:

c121) **9...♗e6** 10 ♕e2 ♗c5 11 ♘c4 ♗g4 12 ♕e1 ♕c7 13 a5 ♖d8 14 ♗e3 0-0 15 f3 ♗c8 16 ♕f2 ♗xe3 17 ♕xe3 ∓ Kindermann-Gerstner, Bundesliga 1992.

c122) **9...♗g4** 10 ♕e1 ♗c5 11 ♘c4 ♕e7 12 h3 ♗h5 13 ♗g5 h6 14 ♗e3 ♘d7 15 a5 f6 16 ♗d2 ♗f7 17 b4 ♗d4 18 c3 ♗a7 19 ♘e3 ± was Milu-Vajda, Odorheiu Secuiesc 1993.

c2) **6...bxc6?!** is never seen nowadays since the following famous game: 7 0-0 d5 8 c4 ♘f6 9 cxd5 cxd5 10 exd5 exd5 11 ♘c3 ♗e7 12 ♕a4+ ♕d7 13 ♖e1 ♕xa4 14 ♘xa4 ♗e6 15 ♗e3 0-0 16 ♗c5 ♖fe8 17 ♗xc7 ♖xe7 18 b4 ♔f8 19 ♘c5 ♗c8 20 f3 ♖ea7 21 ♖e5 ♗d7 22 ♘xd7+ ♖xd7 23 ♖c1 ♖d6 24 ♖c7 ♘d7 25 ♖e2 g6 26 ♔f2 h5 27 f4 h4 28 ♔f3 f5 29 ♔e3 d4+ 30 ♔d2 ♘b6 31 ♖ee7 ♘d5 32 ♖f7+ ♔e8 33 ♖b7 ♘xb4 34 ♗c4 1-0 Fischer-Petrosian, Buenos Aires Ct (7) 1971. This game has supposedly put 6...bxc6 out of business.

6 0-0 ♕c7

6...d6?! used to be the main line but is clearly inflexible and closes the b8-h2 diagonal far too

early. See annotated game 14, Nunn-Gheorghiu.

7 ♕e2 (D)

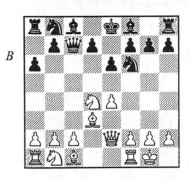

With this move, White signifies his intention of entering the main line of the Kan. Instead of 7 ♕e2, White has played a whole host of other moves: 7 b3, 7 ♔h1, 7 ♗e3, 7 ♘c3, 7 f4?! (7...♗c5! =) and 7 ♘d2. However, all of these moves are not usually played in conjunction with a Maroczy Bind and are therefore discussed in the Scheveningen Systems chapter.

The immediate 7 c4?! is a surprisingly popular move as it is known to give Black equal chances. However, due to its popularity, there is a section devoted to this line.

With 7 ♕e2, White virtually forces Black to play 7...d6. There have been many attempts to retain Black's flexibility but it seems that they are all insufficient:

a) **7...♗c5?!** is the most popular try and was used by Eingorn with some success before White latched on to the best antidote:

a1) **8 ♘b3 ♗a7** (8...♗e7?! 9 e5! ♘d5 10 c4 ♘b4 11 ♗f4 ♘xd3 12 ♕xd3 with a clear advantage to White according to Gurevich):

a11) **9 e5!** ♘d5 10 c4 ♘b4 11 ♗f4 ♘xd3 (11...♘8c6?! 12 ♘1d2 ♘xd3 13 ♕xd3 f5 14 ♕g3 0-0 15 c5! ± was Kudrin-I.Gurevich, Philadelphia 1990) 12 ♕xd3 f6 13 ♕f3! fxe5 14 ♕h5+ g6 15 ♕xe5 ♕xe5 16 ♗xe5 with advantage to White, as in Ulybin-I.Gurevich, Santiago jr Wch 1990.

a12) It seems that 9 e5! is essential, and if White plays 'normally', Black can equalise comfortably, as in Kosashvili-I.Gurevich, Santiago jr Wch 1990: **9 ♗e3 ♗xe3 10 ♕xe3 d6 11 a4 ♘c6 12 ♘1d2 0-0 13 a5 ♗d7 14 ♘d4 ♖ad8!=**.

a2) White should also avoid **8 c3?** when Black can develop freely, as in Coleman-I.Gurevich, London Lloyds Bank 1991: 8...d6 9 ♔h1 ♗d7 10 ♘d2 ♘c6 11 ♘xc6 ♗xc6 12 b4 ♗a7 13 a4 0-0 14 ♗b2 e5 15 ♘f3 ♖fe8 16 c4 a5 17 b5 ♗d7 18 ♘d2 ♗g4!

with a big positional advantage to Black.

b) **7...♗d6?!** seems to be busted after **8 ♔h1!** ♘c6 (8...♗xh2 9 f4 with clear compensation for the pawn) 9 ♘xc6 dxc6 10 f4 ♘d7 11 e5 ♗e7 12 ♗e3 b5 13 ♘d2 ♗b7 14 c4 ♘c5 15 ♗xc5 ♗xc5 16 ♘e4 ♕b6 17 f5 ♗c8 18 f6 g6 19 cxb5 cxb5 20 ♘xc5 ♕xc5 21 ♗e4 ♖b8 22 ♖ac1 ♕a7 23 ♕d2 1-0, as in Van der Wiel-Klinger, Belgrade 1988. In addition, I see nothing wrong with the simple **8 f4 ♗c5 9 c3** when there is no constructive plan apparent for Black.

c) **7...b6!?** was played by Christiansen against Morović but White continued 8 c4, which transposes to the main line, instead of the more critical **8 e5 ♘d5 9 c4 ♘b4 10 ♗e4** with unclear play. 7...b6 needs more practical testing but my instinct is that it is not sufficient.

7 ...   d6 *(D)*

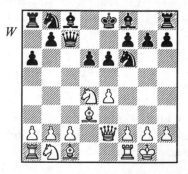

8 c4

Again White has the option of playing a Scheveningen-type system with ♘c3 instead of c4. However, it should be noted that White rarely plays ♕e2 in conjunction with ♘c3 and therefore, since he has 'come this far', it is more likely that he will adopt a Maroczy Bind formation rather than a Scheveningen-type system.

8 f4!? is an attempt to restrain Black from fianchettoing his f8-bishop, and thereby intends to force Black into the Nunn-Gheorghiu games:

a) However, it seems that even here Black can still get away with the fianchetto: **8...g6!?** 9 f5 ♗g7 10 fxe6 fxe6 11 ♗c4 ♘c6 12 ♗e3 ♘xd4 13 ♗xd4 0-0 14 ♘d2 ♗d7 15 c3 ♘h5 16 ♕e3 b5?! 17 ♗b3 ♔h8 18 ♖ad1 ♘f6 19 h3 e5 20 ♗b6 ♕b7 with unclear play, as in M.Schlosser-Vyzhmanavin, Sochi 1989.

b) The other option is to play **8...♘bd7!?** as in Short-Dizdarević, Solingen-Bosna 1988, which continued 9 ♗e3 ♗e7 10 ♘d2 b6 11 c4 ♗b7 12 b4 h5!? 13 ♔h1 h4 14 ♔g1 g6! intending ...e5.

Unfortunately, 8...♘bd7 allows White to play **9 c4!** and Black must then deploy his bishop on e7 instead of g7. White was less successful in Polaczek-Kamsky, Reykjavik 1990 with **9 f4** ♗e7 10 ♘c3 0-0 11 ♘f3 g6 12 ♗e3 b6 13 ♔h1 ♗b7 14 ♗d4 ♘h5 15 ♕d2 ♗f6 16 ♗xf6 ♘dxf6 17 b4 ♖ad8 18 ♖ac1 ♕b8 19 ♘d4 ♖fe8 20 ♘de2 ♕a8 21 ♕c2 ♘g4 22 ♖f3 f5 23 ♘g3 ♘g7 24 h3 ♘f6 25 ♖f2 h5 26 ♖e1 h4 27 ♘f1 ♘gh5 28 ♘d2 ♘g3↑ 29 ♔h2 ♖c8 30 exf5 exf5 31 ♖xe8+ ♖xe8 32 ♘f1 ♕d8 33 ♘xg3 hxg3+ 34 ♔xg3 ♘h5+ 35 ♔h2 ♕h4 36 ♗f1 ♕g3+ 0-1.

c) **8 b3?!** has been played quite often, though it gives Black no problems whatsoever and is played more out of ignorance than anything else. Black can equalise in a number of ways, one example being Dutreeuw-Psakhis, Vienna 1991: 8...g6 9 ♗b2 ♗g7 10 ♘d2 0-0 11 ♔h1 b6 12 f4 ♗b7 13 ♖ae1 ♘bd7 14 e5 ♘h5 15 ♘c4 dxe5 16 fxe5 ♗d5 17 ♘e3 ♗xe5 18 ♘xd5 exd5 19 ♘b5 axb5 20 ♗xe5 ♘xe5 21 ♕xe5 ♕c5 with a slight advantage to Black.

8 ♔h1, 8 ♘c3, 8 ♘d2 and 8 a4 have also been played but are covered in the Scheveningen systems chapter.

Returning to the position after 8 c4 *(D)*:

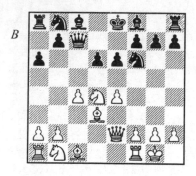

8 ...   g6

This has become the main line of the Sicilian Kan as the previous main line, 8...♗e7, has come into some disrepute as a result of the some Nunn-Gheorghiu clashes in the early 1980s (see annotated game 14).

a) **8...♘bd7** has been seen:

a1) Mainka-Lau, Dortmund 1991 continued **9 ♘c3 ♘e5 10 ♗g5 ♗e7 11 ♖ac1 ♗d7 12 b3 h6 13 ♗h4 ♕c5 14 ♘f3 ♘g6 15 ♖fe1 ♘xh4 16 ♘xh4 0-0** with a comfortable position for Black.

a2) Some players seem to be confused by 8...♘bd7 and Black can trick White into a bad variation of the main line, as in Magem-Prié, Leon 1991: **9 b3?!** g6 10 ♗b2 ♗g7 11 ♘c3 0-0 12 ♖ad1 b6 13 ♗b1 ♗b7 14 ♖fe1 ♖ad8 15 f3 ♖fe8 16 ♕f2 ♕b8 and Black has no problems.

a3) White's best line by far against 8...♘bd7 is to transpose

to the line 1 e4 c5 2 ♘f3 e6 3 d4 cxd4 4 ♘xd4 a6 5 ♗d3 ♘f6 6 0-0 ♕c7 7 ♕e2 d6 8 f4 ♘bd7 by playing **9 f4!** instead of 9 b3?!. See notes to 8 c4 on the previous page for analysis.

b) **8...♘c6!?** is a move which has seen very few outings, e.g. **9 ♘xc6 bxc6 10 ♘c3 ♗e7 11 ♗e3 c5 12 f4** and then:

b1) **12...♗b7** 13 f5! 0-0 14 ♗g5 ♖ae8 15 ♔h1 exf5 16 ♖xf5 ♘d7 17 ♖af1 ♗xg5 18 ♖xg5 ♘e5 as in Ilijin-Barlov, Biel 1989.

b2) **12...0-0** 13 g4 ♗b7 14 g5 ♘d7 15 ♖f3 ♖fe8 16 ♖h3 g6 17 ♕f2 f5 18 ♕h4 ♘f8 19 ♗d2 ♗d8 20 ♖e1 ♕d7 when Black was passive but not clearly worse in Gallagher-Milošević, Geneva 1992.

c) **8...b6** is a speciality of Mortensen but there are only two practical examples of this after **9 ♘c3 ♗b7**:

c1) In Luther-Mortensen, Ostrava 1992, White ignored 8...b6 and simply went down the main line with **10 ♖d1 ♘bd7 11 ♘f3 ♗e7 12 ♗f4 0-0 13 ♖ac1 ♘g4 14 ♗b1 ♘ge5**.

c2) Kan expert, Lev Psakhis, attempted to punish Black for 8...b6 but could only draw after **10 f4 ♗e7 11 ♘f3 0-0 12 ♗d2 ♘bd7 13 b4 a5 14 ♘b5 ♕b8 15 a3 ♖e8 16 ♘bd4 axb4 17 axb4**

♖xa1 18 ♖xa1 e5 19 fxe5 ♘xe5 20 ♘xe5 dxe5 21 ♘f5 ♗f8 22 ♕f3 ♕d8 23 ♖e1 ½-½ Psakhis-Mortensen, Debrecen Echt 1992. Clearly, 10 f4 is the correct way to try to punish 8...b6!? but this interesting move deserves more respect as Black's position is quite resilient.

9 ♘c3   ♗g7 *(D)*

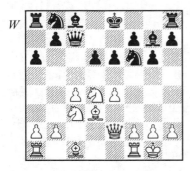

10 ♖d1

This surprising-looking move has become extremely popular in recent years. The idea behind 10 ♖d1 is that since Black has fianchettoed his bishop and thereby removed a possible defender of the d6-pawn, White will simply gang up on this pawn. 'Normal' moves still give a very slight edge to White but are not considered as potent as the text move.

**10 ...   0-0
11 ♘f3**

And White has the simple plan of continuing with ♗f4 and ♗c2, attacking the vulnerable d6-pawn. See main line section of the Kan for annotated games.

The next section deals with an increasingly popular side line in the Kan.

5...♗c5 systems

Game 6
Speelman-Lobron
Munich 1992

1 e4 c5 2 ♘f3 e6 3 d4 cxd4 4 ♘xd4 a6 5 ♗d3 *(D)*

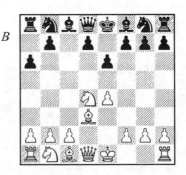

5 ...   ♗c5

The second most popular move and in my opinion, an underrated one. Black gains a tempo for development and places his bishop on a better diagonal than when it is usually placed on e7.

6 ♘b3

The most natural and popular move. Other options include:

a) **6 ♗e3?!** allows Black to develop freely with the simple ...d6 followed by ...♘f6.

b) **6 c3?!** is an equally odd move, which denies White's knight the c3-square and to which Black has many equalising tries. The immediate 6...♘c6 or the more normal development plans of ...d6, ...♘f6, ...♗e7 and 0-0 should both suffice.

6 ...   ♗a7

6...♗b6 is also playable but it makes little or no difference as White will eventually challenge the black bishop by playing ♗e3 in which case Black usually exchanges bishops.

A very rarely seen plan and one which I think has some good ideas behind it is **6...♗e7!?**. The idea of this simple bishop retreat is not new and is in fact one of the main lines of the Scheveningen-type systems (see Chapter 4). The point behind the move is that if White plays the immediate 7 c4, with a Maroczy Bind, the knight on b3 is slightly misplaced whereas Black has made no such concessions. Also, if White plays 7 ♘c3 with a Scheveningen-type formation, the knight on d4 has been driven away to b3, which can only be advantageous for Black.

The only question is if White can take immediate advantage of 6...♗e7 with 7 ♕g4!?. Recent games are of no theoretical help as White has only played 7 0-0 and 7 ♘c3.

7 ♕e2 (D)

The most direct way. Others:

a) **7 0-0** is good for a small advantage but hardly critical: 7...♘e7 8 ♕e2 ♘bc6 9 ♗e3 ♗xe3 10 ♕xe3 0-0 11 ♘c3 d5 12 exd5 exd5 13 ♘e2 ♖e8 14 ♖fe1 ♘g6 15 ♕g3 ♕e7 16 ♗xg6 hxg6 17 ♕c3 ♗f5 18 ♕d2 ♕f6 19 ♘bd4 ♖e4 20 c3 ♖ae8 21 ♖ed1 ♘e5 22 ♘g3 ♖h4 23 ♖e1 ♗d7 24 ♖ad1 ♖h6 25 ♘f1 ♔h7 26 b3 g5 27 ♖e3 ½-½ D.Barbulescu-Kirov, Havana 1986. Of course, Black has a number of other options and does not have to play as in the above.

b) **7 ♕g4** does not win a pawn after **7...♘f6!** as **8 ♕xg7?** is met with 8...♖g8 followed by ...♖xg2 and Black is attacking f2. However, it is possible to play in the following manner: **8 ♕g3!?** d6 9 ♘c3 ♘c6 10 0-0 b5 11 ♔h1 ♗b7 (Black played too ambitiously in Mainka-I.Stang, Bundesliga 1993, with 11...b4?! 12 ♘e2 e5? 13 ♗g5 h6 14 ♗xf6 ♕xf6 15 ♗c4! 0-0 16 ♕d3 ♘e7 17 a3! bxa3 18 ♖xa3 ♗c5 19 ♘xc5 dxc5 ±) 12 f4 0-0

13 ♗d2 ♔h8 14 ♖ac1 ♘b4 15 f5
♘xd3 16 cxd3 =, as in Van der
Weide-Smejkal, Amsterdam
1971.

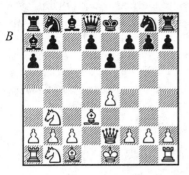

7 ...   ♘c6

Previously played moves include 7...♘e7 8 ♗e3 ♗xe3 9
♕xe3 ♘bc6 10 ♘c3 b5 11 e5 d6
12 exd6 ♕xd6 13 0-0-0 ♕e5 14
♗e4 ♗b7 15 ♘c5 ♖b8 16 ♘d7
♘d5 17 ♘xe5 ♘xe3 18 ♘xc6
♗xc6 19 fxe3 1-0 A.Holmsten-
Nunez, World jr Ch 1990.

8 ♗e3   d6
9 ♘c3   ♘f6!? (D)

9...♗xe3 is a major alternative.
See next annotated game.
9...♘ge7!? is an interesting idea
which needs more practical testing. In West-Christiansen, Philadelphia World Open 1990, White
played as if the knight were on f6
and soon obtained an inferior position after 10 0-0-0 0-0 11 h4 b5
12 ♖dg1 b4 13 ♘d1 a5 14 ♔b1
a4 15 ♘d2 ♘e5 ∓.

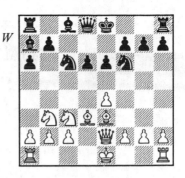

10 0-0-0

Or **10 f4** (instead after 10 ♗xa7
♖xa7, 11 f4 e5 transposes, but
White could try 11 g4!?) **10...e5!
11 ♗xa7 ♖xa7 12 f5 b5** and now:

a) **13 0-0** ♘e7 14 a4 b4 15 ♘d1
0-0 16 a5 d5 17 exd5 ♖e8 18 ♘e3
♘exd5 19 ♘xd5 ♕xd5 was
Gavrikov-Christiansen, Biel
1991 and Black had the advantage.

b) White did no better in Ste-
fansson-Christiansen, Manila
OL 1992: **13 ♕e3** 0-0 14 a4 b4 15
♘d5 ♘xd5 16 exd5 ♘d4 17
♘xd4 exd4 18 ♕xd4 ♖e7+ 19
♔f2 ♖e5 20 ♖he1 ♗xf5 21 ♖xe5
dxe5 22 ♕xe5 ♗xd3 23 cxd3
♖e8 with a clear advantage to
Black though the game was actually drawn in 59 moves.

c) Perhaps White's best is **13
0-0-0** 0-0 14 g4 ♘d4 15 ♕g2 b4
16 ♘e2 ♘xe2+ 17 ♗xe2 a5 18
♘d2 ♗a6 19 g5 ♘d7 20 ♗xa6
♖xa6 21 ♘c4 a4 22 ♔b1 ♕c7 23
♘e3 b3 24 cxb3 axb3 25 a3 ♘c5

26 ♘d5 ♕b7 27 ♖he1 ♖a4 28 ♘f6+ ♔h8 29 ♘xh7 1-0, as in Yudasin-Nikolaev, Podolsk 1991.

10 ...   b5! *(D)*

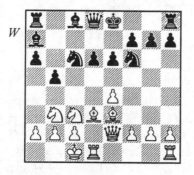

11   ♗xa7

11 f4 b4 12 ♘a4 ♗d7 13 ♗xa7? ♘xa7! – Speelman.

11 ...   ♖xa7

12   f4

12 g4!? resulted in a win for White in Arnason-Motwani, Hafnarfirdi 1992: 12...0-0 13 f4 b4 14 ♘a4 ♘e7 15 g5 ♘e8 16 ♕f2 ♕c7 17 ♘b6 a5 18 ♘xc8 ♘xc8 19 ♘d4 ♕b6 20 ♖hf1 ♖c7 21 ♔b1 a4 22 f5 e5 23 ♘b5 ♖c5 24 c4 d5?! 25 exd5 ♘cd6 26 ♘xd6 ♘xd6 27 f6 e4 28 fxg7 ♖b8 29 ♗xe4 b3 30 ♖d3 ♖xc4 31 ♗xh7+ ♔xg7 32 ♕f6+ ♔f8 33 g6 ♖g4 34 ♖e1 ♘e4 1-0.

12 ...   b4

13   ♘a4

This knight is the cause of all Black's counterplay in this game.

However, after **13 ♘b1?!**, Black's queenside attack is very fast after ...0-0 and ...a5-a4.

13 ...   e5!

The standard idea in this system. Once Black is rid of his dark-squared bishop, he can safely play this move. As in most of the Sicilian examples where Black plays ...e5, the move is less potent with the bishop on e7.

14   f5   0-0

15   g4   ♗d7

15...♘d4? 16 ♘xd4 exd4 17 ♕f2 ±.

16   g5   ♘e8

17   ♕e3   ♖b7!

18   ♗xa6   ♖b8 *(D)*

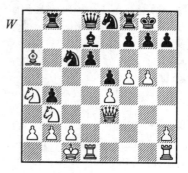

19   ♔b1

Two recent games have seen big improvements for White:

a) 19 ♕d2 ♘e7 20 ♘ac5 ♗c6 21 ♗c4 ♕c8 22 f6 ♘g6 23 ♘a6 ♖a8 24 ♘xb4 was ± in Stefansson-Schlosser, Altensteig 1992.

**b) 19 ♗c4! ♔h8 20 ♕d2 ♘a5
21 ♘xa5 ♕xa5 22 b3 ♖c8 23
♕d5 ♕a7 24 ♔b1 ♕e3 25 ♖he1
♕xg5 26 ♘b6 ♗c6 27 ♕a5 ♕d8
28 ♗d5 ♗xd5 29 ♖xd5 ♖c6 30
♘c4 ♕h4 31 ♕xb4** was again ±
in Yakovich-Emms, Cappelle la
Grande 1993.

19 ... ♕c7!

Ever patient, Black correctly
realises that the knight on a4 will
not run away.

20 ♖d5 ♘e7

It was possible to win a piece
by **20...♘d4 21 ♘xd4 exd4 22
♖xd4 ♗xa4** but White has some
counterplay after 23 g6! and
♗c4.

**21 ♖a5 ♘xf5!
22 exf5 ♗xa4
23 ♖xa4** *(D)*

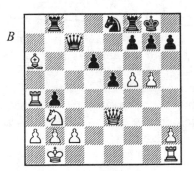

23 ... ♕c6!

A remarkable tactic which nets
Black the exchange.

**24 ♖d1 ♕xa4
25 ♗c4 ♖c8**

**26 ♘d2 ♕c6
27 ♗b3 ♘c7**

27...♕g2 intending 28 ♘e4?
d5! is also good for Black.

**28 ♘c4 ♘b5
29 ♘b6 ♘d4!
30 ♘xc8 ♕xc8**

If **30...♖xc8** then 31 g6!.

31 ♖f1?

31 g6 would have caused Black
more problems.

**31 ... ♕a6!
32 ♖f2 ♕c6
33 ♕e1 ♘xb3!?**

Speelman gives **33...♖a8!** 34
g6 ♘xb3 35 gxf7+ ♔xf7 36 cxb3
(36 axb3 ♕a6 37 ♔c1 ♕a1+ 38
♔d2 ♕xb2 with a winning advantage for Black) 36...♕a6 37
♕xb4 ♕a2+ 38 ♔c2 ♖c8+ 39
♔d3 ♕b1+ (39... ♕a6+ is also
possible) 40 ♔e3 ♕c1+ and
White will soon be mated.

**34 axb3 ♖a8
35 ♕e2! ♕c5
36 g6 ♕a7
37 ♔c1 d5?**

a) **37...e4?** 38 gxf7+ ♔xf7 39
♕xe4 and White is fine.

b) **37...♕d4!** 38 gxf7+ (38
♔b1? e4 39 gxf7+ ♔xf7 40 ♕c4+
♕xc4 41 bxc4 ♔f6 ∓) 38...♔f8!
(38...♔xf7 39 ♕c4+ ♕xc4 40
bxc4) 39 ♔b1 d5! (39...e4 40
♕d2!) 40 ♕d2 ♕xd2 41 ♖xd2
♖a5 and Black has a clear advantage in the endgame.

38	gxf7+	♔xf7
39	♕xe5!=	♕xf2
40	♕e6+	♔f8
41	♕d6+	♔e8
42	♕e6+	♔f8

½-½

Notes based on analysis by Speelman.

In the next game, Black does not delay in capturing the white bishop on e3.

Game 7
Short-Velikov
Bundesliga 1987

1 e4 c5 2 ♘f3 e6 3 d4 cxd4 4 ♘xd4 a6 5 ♗d3 ♗c5 6 ♘b3 ♗a7 7 ♕e2 ♘c6 8 ♗e3 (D)

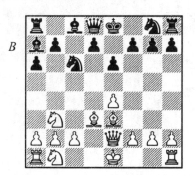

| 8 | ... | ♗xe3 |

Contrary to the Speelman-Lobron game, Black decides to exchange bishops immediately.

| 9 | ♕xe3 | ♘f6 |

| 10 | ♘c3 | d6 |
| 11 | 0-0-0 | |

White could castle kingside but the dark-squared bishop exchange favours Black in these type of positions. Black would simply castle himself and play a timely ...e5! with full equality.

| 11 | ... | 0-0 |
| 12 | f4 | ♕c7 *(D)* |

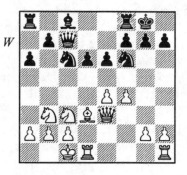

13 g4!?

It is still not clear if White needs to prepare this move with ♖hg1 or ♕h3 though 13 g4!? is now considered the main line of this variation. In each case, it is fair to say that White retains a small advantage.

a) **13 ♖hg1 b5 14 g4 b4 15 g5:**
a1) **15...♘e8 16 ♘b1 a5 17 ♖g4 a4 18 ♘3d2 ♗a6 19 ♗xa6 ♖xa6 20 ♖h4 g6 21 ♕h3 f5 22 gxf6 ♖xf6 23 ♘c4** was better for White in Wedberg-Spraggett, New York 1987.

a2) **15...♘d7** 16 ♘e2 a5 17 ♔b1 ♗a6 18 h4 a4 19 ♘bd4 ♕b6 20 ♗xa6 ♖xa6 21 ♕h3 ♕c7 22 g6 ♘xd4 23 gxh7+ ♔xh7 24 ♖xg7+ ♔h8 25 ♘xd4 ♖aa8 26 ♖g5 ♘f6 27 e5 dxe5 28 fxe5 ♘h7 29 ♕g4 f5 30 exf6 e5 31 ♖g1 ♘xf6 32 ♕f5 1-0 was a crushing win for White in Yudasin-Suetin, Leipzig 1986.

b) **13 ♕h3 b5 14 g4** and now:

b1) After **14...g6** White mishandled the position in Kindermann-Lobron, Bundesliga 1983: 15 g5 ♘h5 16 ♕e3 b4 17 ♘e2 a5 18 ♔b1 a4 19 ♘bd4 ♕a7 20 ♗b5 ♘e7 21 ♕d2 ♕c5 22 c4 ♗b7 23 ♕d3 e5 24 ♘f3 exf4 25 ♖he1 a3 with an advantage to Black.

b2) A more direct attempt by White seems to be the best try but Bronstein could only draw after **14...♘b4** 15 g5 ♘xd3+ 16 ♖xd3 ♘e8 17 f5 b4 18 ♕h4 bxc3 19 ♖h3 cxb2+ 20 ♔b1 f6 21 ♕xh7+ ♔f7 22 ♖g1 ♖g8 23 ♖h6 exf5 24 ♖xf6+ ♘xf6 25 gxf6 ♔xf6 26 ♕xg8 ♗b7 27 ♕h7 ♗xe4 28 ♕g6+ ♔e5 29 ♕g3+ ½-½ in Bronstein-Suetin, Moscow 1982.

Returning to the position after 13 g4 *(D)*:

13 ...   ♘xg4?!

It would take a brave man to repeat this dubious acceptance of the sacrifice after the outcome of this game.

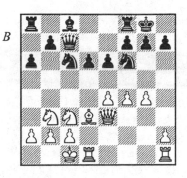

Now, Black nearly always plays the safer **13...b5**, as in Kengis-Nevednichy, USSR 1979 which went 14 g5 ♘d7 15 f5 b4 16 ♘e2 a5 17 ♕h3 exf5 18 exf5 ♘de5 19 ♘f4 a4 20 ♘d5 ♕d8 21 ♖hg1 ♘xd3+ 22 ♖xd3 ♘e5 23 ♘f6+ gxf6 24 ♕h6 ♘xd3+ 25 ♔b1 fxg5 26 f6 ♕xf6 27 ♕xf6 g4 28 ♕g5+ ♔h8 29 ♕f6+ ♔g8 30 ♘d4 ♘e5 31 h3 h5 32 ♕g5+ ♘g6 33 ♕xh5 gxh3 34 ♕d5 ♗e6 35 ♘xe6 h2 36 ♖xg6+ 1-0. See *Beating the Sicilian 3* by John Nunn and Joe Gallagher for detailed analysis of this game.

14 ♕g3   ♘f6
15 ♖hg1   ♘e8

Nobody seems to have played **15...g6** though I cannot see anything terribly wrong with it. The immediate 16 f5?! would give Black the sole use of the e5-square and White would do better to play 16 h4 with the idea of a future h4-h5. Nevertheless, whatever Black's continuation, it is clear that White has good compensation for the sacrificed pawn.

16 ♔b1

16 f5 f6 (16...♘e5?! 17 f6! ±; 16...d5?! 17 exd5 exd5 18 ♘xd5 ♕xg3 19 ♖xg3 ±) was seen in Dekar-Hallier, corr. 1990 and after 17 ♗c4 ♘d8 18 fxe6 ♗xe6 19 ♗d5 ♗xd5 20 ♘xd5 ♕f7 21 ♘d4 ♔h8 22 ♘f5 ♘c6 23 ♕h4 ♘e5 24 ♖g3 ♖d8 25 ♖f1 g6 26 ♘fe3 ♕g7 27 ♘f5, White was excellently placed.

16 ... ♘e7?!

Too passive. Better was **16...b5**, preparing a future counter-attack.

17 ♘d4 ± ♕c5

17...e5 fails to 18 ♘f5! ♗xf5 19 exf5 intending f6, e.g. 19 ...exf4 (19...♔h8 20 f6 gxf6 21 ♗xh7!) 20 ♕xf4 d5 21 ♕h4 f6 22 ♘xd5! ♘xd5 23 ♗c4 ±.

18 ♘f3 f6 *(D)*

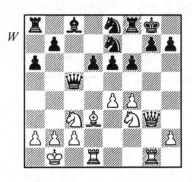

19 e5!

White opens the floodgates.

19 ... dxe5

19...d5 20 ♕h4 f5 21 ♘g5 h6 22 ♕xh6!! gxh6 23 ♘xe6+ ♕xg1 24 ♖xg1+ ♘g7 (24...♔f7 25 ♘d8#; 24...♔h8 25 ♘xf8+-) 25 ♖xg7+ ♔h8 26 ♖xe7+-.

20 fxe5 f5

21 ♕h4 ♕c7

21...♘g6 22 ♖xg6 hxg6 23 ♘g5 ♖f7 24 ♗c4! (24 ♕h7+ ♔f8 25 ♕h8+ ♔e7 26 ♘xf7 ♔xf7 27 ♘e4 ♕xe5 28 ♘g5+ ♔e7 29 ♘h7 ♗d7!) ♕xe5 25 ♖d8+-.

21...b5 22 ♘g5 h6 23 ♕xh6 gxh6 24 ♘xe6+ ♕xg1 25 ♖xg1+ ±.

22 ♗c4! h6

23 ♕xh6! ♕xc4

24 ♖xg7+! ♘xg7

25 ♘g5

25 ♖g1? ♕g4!.

25 ... ♖e8

26 ♖g1 *(D)*

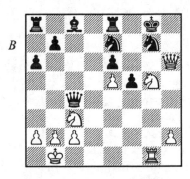

26 ... ♕d4

26...♘d5 27 ♘xe6 or **26...♕g4 27 ♖xg4 fxg4 28 ♘ce4.**

27	♕h7+	♔f8
28	♘xe6+	♘xe6
29	♕h6+	**1-0**

Notes based on analysis by Minić and Sindić in *Informator 43*.

We now turn our attention to the main line of the Kan and one where there have been new developments.

**Main-line Kan;
White allows ...e5!?
Game 8
Stefansson-Lutz**
Manila OL 1992

1 e4 c5 2 ♘f3 e6 3 d4 cxd4 4 ♘xd4 a6 5 ♗d3 ♕c7 6 0-0 ♘f6 7 ♕e2 d6 8 c4 g6 9 ♘c3 ♗g7 10 ♖d1 0-0 11 ♘f3 *(D)*

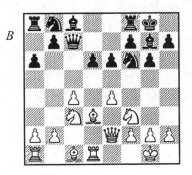

| **11** | ... | **♘c6!?** |

An unusual move to play in the Hedgehog as with the queen on c7 and the knight on c6, Black can run into problems on the c-file. An idea for White would be simply to develop his queen's bishop, play his queen's rook to c1 and then the standard ♘d5! would give him a clear advantage.

Of course, Black will not allow this and 11...♘c6 is based on a cunning equalising trick.

12 ♗f4 *(D)*

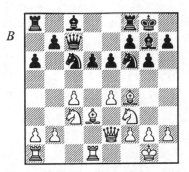

| **12** | ... | **e5!!** |

An incredible decision which seemingly weakens d5 for no compensation. However, Black has correctly calculated that White will also have problems with his d4-square and therefore the two weaknesses cancel each other out.

Only now do we see the point of 11...♘c6. From c6 the knight can go to d4 and thereby justify the move 12...e5!!. Note also that one possible line goes 11...♘bd7 12 ♗f4 ♘e5 and that in the above diagram, instead of 12...e5!!, Black still has the option of transposing to this option with 12...♞e5.

In fact 12 ♗f4 is an inaccuracy by White and the game Luther-Stefansson (see annotated game 9) shows an improvement for White which forces Black to play an alternative line. Had Black played the more normal 12...♞fd7 (to play ...♞de5, blockading the h2-b8 diagonal), White would then continue 13 h3! thus putting a stop to all of Black's ...e5 ideas.

13 ♗e3

13 ♗g5 was seen in Luther-Farago, Budapest Elekes 1991 but after 13...♗g4 14 ♖ac1 ♞d4 15 ♕e3 ♗xf3 16 gxf3 h6 17 ♗xh6 ♗xh6 18 ♕xh6 ♞xf3+ 19 ♔g2 ♞d4 20 ♞d5 ♕d8 21 ♖g1 ♞xd5 22 exd5 ♕f6 Black had a clear advantage and went on to win in 45 moves.

13 ...   ♗g4 (D)

A vital ingredient. Black must remove one of the defenders of the d4-square.

14 ♗c2!?

After **14 h3, 14...♞d4** 15 ♗xd4 exd4 16 ♞d5 ♗xf3 17 ♕xf3 was Almasi-Farago, Hungarian Ch 1992 and the players agreed a draw in this totally equal position.

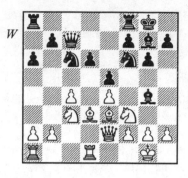

A more ambitious plan was used by Stefansson, this time as Black: **14...♗xf3** 15 ♕xf3 ♞d7 16 ♞d5 ♕d8 17 b4 ♞d4 18 ♕g3 ♞f6 19 ♗g5 ♞e6 with a more double-edged but nonetheless equal game; Kotronias-Stefansson, Komotini Grand Prix 1993.

14 ...   ♞d7

Black strangely gives up all form of protection over the d5-square but he has correctly calculated that White can also do very little about his own weakness on d4. The knight will now head to e6 via c5.

15	♞d5	♕d8
16	h3	♗xf3
17	♕xf3	♞c5
18	♕e2	

18 ♗xc5 dxc5 would merely accentuate the problem on d4 as White has no good discovered attack.

18	...	♞e6
19	♕d2	♞cd4
20	♗d3	♖b8

21 f3

With such a glaring weakness on d5, Black will have difficulty in going all-out for a win. However, White's own weakness on d4 and the fact that Black can try to undermine White's grip on d5 by the pawn breaks ...b5 and ...f5, ensure Black an active game.

21	...	f5
22	exf5	gxf5
23	♖f1	♔h8
24	♖ad1	b5

The second phase of the undermining process. Notice how White's grip on d5 is gradually removed.

25	cxb5	axb5
26	♖c1	♕d7
27	♗b1 (D)	

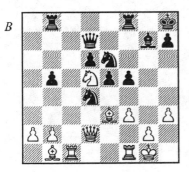

27 ... ♕b7!

And finally the white knight is driven away. Had Black waited one more move, e.g. **27...♖bc8?**, White would have countered with 28 a3! with the idea of ♗a2, protecting the knight on d5.

28	♘b4	♖bc8?!

The c-file is of little importance in this position and Black should have played **28...♖bd8!** intending to answer 29 ♘c2 with 29...♘xc2 30 ♗xc2 d5! with a massive centre and a protected passed pawn. The text move allows White to liquidate, which is to his advantage.

29	♖xc8!	♖xc8
30	♘c2!	♕f7

Forced in order to protect the f-pawn which Black 'undefended' by allowing the exchange of rooks.

31	♘xd4	exd4
32	♗f4	♕f8
33	♗d3	♖c5 (D)

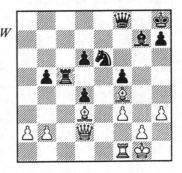

34	b4	♖c4
35	♗h2	♗h6
36	f4?	

A bad move which hinders the dark-squared bishop for no reason. **36 ♕b2** would have assured White some advantage.

36	...	♕f6
37	a4	d5!
38	axb5	♗f8
39	♗xc4 *(D)*	

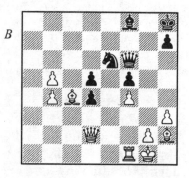

39	...	dxc4

Thanks to White's careless 36th move, Black has just enough time to create counterplay with his two connected passed pawns. Nevertheless, White should still win.

40 ♕c2 c3 41 b6 ♘g7 42 b7 ♕b6 43 ♕d3 ♕xb7 44 ♕xd4 ♕xb4 45 ♕xb4 ♗xb4 46 ♖c1 ♘e6 47 ♔f1 ♘c5 48 ♗g1 ♘d3 49 ♖c2 ♘xf4 50 ♗d4+ ♔g8 51 ♗xc3 ♘d5 52 ♗xb4??

A blunder which throws away the win. Either 52 ♗d4 or ♗d2 would have won the game eventually.

52...♘e3+ 53 ♔e2 ♘xc2 54 ♗c5 f4 55 ♔d2 ♘e3 56 ♗xe3 fxe3+ 57 ♔xe3 ♔f7 58 ♔f4 ♔f6

59 g4 ♔g6 60 h4 ♔f6 61 g5+ ♔g6 62 ♔g4 h6 63 h5+ ♔g7 64 g6 ♔g8 ½-½

A tense game where both sides had chances to win.

The following game is a more accurate way of playing the system for White, but again Black can play for activity.

Game 9
Luther-Stefansson
Altensteig 1992

1 e4 c5 2 ♘f3 e6 3 d4 cxd4 4 ♘xd4 a6 5 ♗d3 ♘f6 6 0-0 ♕c7 7 ♕e2 d6 8 c4 g6 9 ♘c3 ♗g7 10 ♖d1 0-0 11 ♘f3 ♘c6 *(D)*

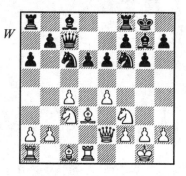

12 h3!

A clever move, which denies Black the chance to play his equalising line of **12 ♗f4?! e5!**. Black is now forced to play one of the old main lines.

12	...	♘d7

13 ♗f4   ♘ce5

13...e5? would now be a mistake as Black can never play ...♗g4, exchanging the bishop for the more useful knight.

14 ♖ac1   b6
15 b3   ♗b7
16 ♗b1 *(D)*

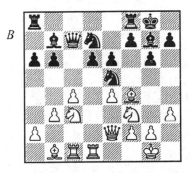

16 ...   f5!?

An interesting alternative to the more usual Hedgehog plans. Unfortunately, due to the dark-squared bishop being on g7, Black has some difficulties in carrying out the more routine Hedgehog ideas. For example **16...♖ac8** 17 ♘xe5 ♘xe5 18 ♕d2 ♖fd8 19 ♗g5! and Black would then either have to play the unnatural **19...♖d7** or the ugly **19...f6?!**. One other idea would be to try to deny the g5-square from the white bishop with **16...h6** intending to answer 17 ♘xe5 ♘xe5 18 ♕d2 with 18...g5 though after the simple bishop

retreat 19 ♗g3, White has an undisputed advantage.

17 ♘d4   ♖ae8
18 ♕d2 *(D)*

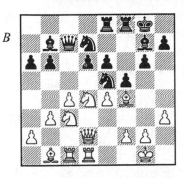

18 ...   ♘f7!

A very important move which not only defends the weak d6-pawn but also guards the dark squares on the kingside. Currently, there is little or no established theory on this particular line but my experience with these particular type of Hedgehog positions is that Black needs to have some control over the c1-h6 diagonal.

Although it may seem that this diagonal is not of vital importance, often Black is harassed along this diagonal by the white bishop on e3 either by ♗g5 or ♗h6. The knight on f7 adds vital protection to these squares, thereby setting up the opportunity to play ...h6 and perhaps, at a later stage, ...g5.

I would say that the above position is roughly equal. It should be noted though that Black is justifying his flimsy pawn structure tactically and White's pieces are more harmoniously placed. The immediate threat is ...e5, winning a piece.

19	♘de2	e5
20	♗h2	♗h6
21	f4	fxe4
22	♗xe4	♗xe4
23	♘xe4	exf4
24	♘2c3	

White has no choice but to allow ...f4-f3 as he has no way to blockade the f4-square. The knight on e2 might as well head for d5.

24	...	f3!

The f-pawn will be the source of compensation for all of Black's positional drawbacks.

25	♗f4	♗xf4
26	♕xf4	♘fe5
27	♕g3	♘c5
28	♖xd6?!	

28 ♘xd6 f2+ 29 ♔f1! was better.

28	...	♔h8
29	♖f1	b5
30	cxb5	axb5
31	♔h2	♘xe4
32	♘xe4	♖f5
33	♖f6?!	

33 gxf3 ♘xf3+ 34 ♖xf3 ♖xe4 35 ♖d2 =.

33	...	♕e7
34	♖xf5?	gxf5
35	♘g5	♖g8
36	♖e1	♖xg5
37	♕xe5+	♕xe5+
38	♖xe5	f2!

0-1

Game 10
Anand-Kamsky
Delhi 1990

1 e4 c5 2 f3 e6 3 d4 cxd4 4 ♘xd4 a6 5 ♗d3 ♘f6 6 0-0 ♕c7 7 ♕e2 d6 8 c4 g6 9 ♖d1 ♗g7 10 ♘f3 ♘c6 11 ♗f4 0-0 12 ♗c2?! *(D)*

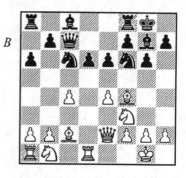

12	...	e5!

Again White has been inaccurate. After 12 h3!, Black would have had to play 12...♘fd7 13 ♗c2 ♘de5.

13 ♗e3

We already know about the equalising method via 13...♗g4.

In this position, Black has an even better option.

13 ...   ♘b4!

Forcing White to give up the bishop pair.

14 ♘c3   ♘xc2
15 ♕xc2   ♕xc4 *(D)*

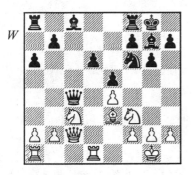

16 ♖xd6

Although material is equal, White has lost his Maroczy Bind and Black has the advantage of the two bishops.

16 ...   b5!
17 ♗b6

Not 17 ♘xe5?? ♕c7!.

17 ...   ♗b7

17...b4? 18 ♘d2 ± – Anand.

18 ♘d2   ♕c8?!

Black should prefer 18...♕b4! when after 19 ♖d3 ♖fc8 White has lost all his opening move advantage. If instead 19 ♕d3 then 19...♕xb2 20 ♖b1 ♕a3 and it is not clear what compensation White has for the sacrificed pawn.

19 ♕d3

With his last move, Black has allowed White to centralise and now begins a dubious kingside attack.

19 ...   ♘h5
20 g3   ♕h3
21 ♘d5   ♔h8
22 ♕f1!   ♕xf1+
23 ♘xf1   f5
24 ♖d1   ♘f6

It is clear that Black has lost much of his early initiative, and White's control of d5 gives him a clear edge. If instead 24...fxe4?!, then 25 ♘fe3 ♘f6 26 ♘c7 with a clear advantage.

25 ♘xf6   ♗xf6
26 exf5   gxf5
27 ♖d7   ♗e4

27...♗c6?! 28 ♖c7 ♖ac8? 29 ♖d6 ♖xc7 30 ♗xc7 ♗e4 31 ♖xf6!±.

28 ♘e3   ♖ac8
29 b4   ♗f3
30 ♖e1   f4
31 ♘f1! *(D)*

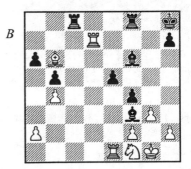

31 ...   **♗g7**

A more active option would have been **31...♖c2**.

32	♘d2	♗g4
33	♖a7	♖c2
34	♘e4	♖xa2
35	♗c5	♖d8
36	♗e7!	♖e2
37	♖f1	♖c8
38	♗f6!	♗xf6 (D)

If **38...♖g8**, then 39 ♘g5! (39 ♗xg7+ ♖xg7 40 ♖a8 ♖g8 41 ♖xg8+ ♔xg8 42 ♘f6+ ♔g7 43 ♘xg4 h5=) 39...h6 40 ♘f7+ ♔h7 41 ♘xe5 with a clear advantage to White.

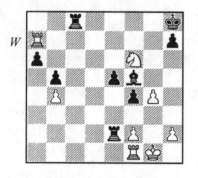

39	♘xf6	♗f5
40	g4!	♖f8?

The final, and decisive mistake. **40...♗e4!** is necessary:

a) **41 ♖d1 ♖d2!** 42 ♖a1 ♖a2 and White can make no headway.

b) **41 f3 ♗g6** and Black has enough time to untangle his pieces.

c) **41 h4!** h6 42 g5 ♖d8 43 ♔h2 ♖c8 (not 44...hxg5? 45 hxg5 ♖c8 46 ♖h1!!) 44 ♔h3 ♗f5+ 45 ♔g2 ♗e4+ with unclear play.

41 ♖d1!!   **♗g6**

If now **41...♗e4** then either 42 ♔f1 or 42 f3 would give White a clear advantage.

42	♖dd7	♖e1+
43	♔g2	f3+
44	♔h3	1-0

Notes based on analysis by Anand.

The games so far have seen a fresh approach to the problems that Black faces in these types of Hedgehog positions. The next game is an example of the older approach to these problems and though it has not been completely discarded, there is no doubt that White has an easy game:

Game 11
Gallagher-I.Gurevich
London Lloyds Bank 1992

1 e4 c5 2 ♘f3 e6 3 d4 cxd4 4 ♘xd4 a6 5 ♗d3 ♕c7 6 0-0 ♘f6 7 ♕e2 d6 8 c4 g6 9 ♘c3 ♗g7 10 ♖d1 0-0 11 ♗c2 (D) 11...♘bd7

The older move that Kan players nearly always played. With the introduction of the ...e5 idea, Black now knows that the knight is better placed on c6.

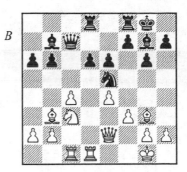

12 ♘f3   ♘g4

13 ♗f4   ♘ge5

Seeking immediate activity with **13...♘de5** is too ambitious: 14 ♘d2! b5 (14...b6 is better – Cabrilo) 15 h3 ♘f6 16 cxb5 axb5 17 ♗b3 b4 18 ♘b5 ♕b8 19 ♘xd6 ♘h5 20 ♗xe5 ♗xe5 21 ♘2c4 ± was Cabrilo-Kovačević, Vrnjačka Banja 1988.

14 ♗b3!?

Equally viable is **14 ♘xe5 ♘xe5 15 b3** followed by ♖ac1 and ♕d2. However, occasionally, with the white pawns on a2, b3 and c4 the light-squared bishop is hemmed in. The text move is an interesting attempt at improving this troublesome piece.

14 ...   b6

15 ♘xe5   ♘xe5

16 ♗g3   ♗b7

17 ♖ac1   ♖ad8

18 f3 *(D)*

18 ...   ♔h8?!

The start of an ambitious plan. The problem with the old main line is perfectly highlighted in the above diagram. White has nothing more than a comfortable advantage but Black will find it very hard to do anything creative. As this game shows, the minute that Black starts an ambitious plan, White's harmoniously placed pieces 'take care of the position'.

19 ♗f2   f5?!

Black simply has too many weaknesses (on b6, d6 and e6) to defend after this move.

20 ♗d4   fxe4

Black would have preferred **20...f4** with the compensation that he has total control of e5 and chances of a kingside attack with ...g5 and ...g4. However, White has the immediate shot 21 ♕f2 ♘d7 22 ♘a4, which simply wins a pawn.

21 ♘xe4 *(D)*

21 ...   Rf4?

The losing move, though it is already hard to suggest a better alternative.

22 Be3   Rf5
23 c5!

The previously troublesome light-squared bishop is now activated and Black's task is hopeless.

23 ...   bxc5
24 Bxe6   Rff8
25 Bd5!±   Bxd5
26 Rxd5   Nc6
27 Qd2!   Qb8

27...Nb4? was impossible due to the indirect attack on the black queen by the rook on c1. The rest of the game is not instructive.

28 Rxd6 Be5 29 Bxc5 Bxd6 30 Bxd6 Qa7+ 31 Kh1 Ne7 32 Qc3+ Kg8 33 Qb3+ Kg7 34 Rc7 Qd4 35 Qc3 Qxc3 36 Rxe7+ Rf7 37 Rxf7+ Kxf7 38 bxc3 Rd7 39 Kg1 Rb7 40 Bb4 1-0

White is not limited to the approach highlighted so far in the main line. Instead, he has the option of playing more 'classically'.

Other main-line options for White

Game 12
Almasi-Vogt
Altensteig 1993

1 e4 c5 2 Nf3 e6 3 d4 cxd4 4 Nxd4 a6 5 Bd3 Nf6 6 0-0 Qc7 7 Qe2 d6 8 c4 g6 9 Nc3 Bg7 10 Nf3 0-0 11 Rd1 Nc6 12 h3 Nd7 *(D)*

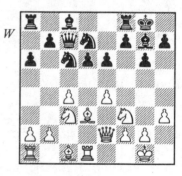

13 Be3!?

An interesting alternative to the more usual 13 Bf4, which is enough to give White a slight edge.

13 ...   b6
14 Rac1   Bb7
15 Bb1

If now **15 ♘d5** then simply 15...♕d8! forces the knight to return to c3. In other Hedgehog positions, however, Black's dark-squared bishop is on e7 and White would simply net the two bishops with ♘xe7+ instead of having to retreat to c3. Here of course, the bishop is safely on g7.

15	...	♘ce5
16	♘xe5	♘xe5
17	b3 *(D)*	

17 f4?! ♘xc4 18 ♘a4 ♕b8 19 ♖xc4 b5 gives Black the initiative. In the style of Karpov, White prefers to consolidate his spatial advantage.

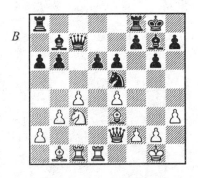

17	...	♖fd8
18	♕d2	♗f8
19	♘a4	♘d7
20	♗g5	♖db8!

Unfortunately, the more natural **20...♖e8?** is bad due to 21 ♗f4 ♘e5 22 ♕d4 and Black cannot defend all his weak points. This usually happens in the Hedgehog

when a pair of minor pieces are exchanged.

| 21 | ♘c3 | ♖e8 |

Once the white knight stops menacing the b-pawn, the black rook returns to the more natural e8-square.

22	♗h4	♖ac8
23	♗g3	♘e5
24	f4	♘c6

24...♘d7? fails to 25 e5! with a winning advantage to White.

25	♗f2	♖b8
26	a3	♗a8
27	b4	♕e7 *(D)*

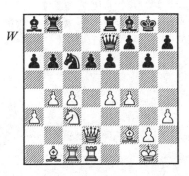

28 ♘a4!

After this, White has a clear advantage as Black has not managed to tee up either of the traditional Hedgehog pawn breaks, ...d5 or ...b5. **28...b5** is not a viable option as after the simple 29 cxb5 axb5 30 ♘c3, White will simply play ♗d3 followed by ♕e2, with unbearable pressure against the b5-pawn.

28	...	♛d8
29	♗e3 *(D)*	

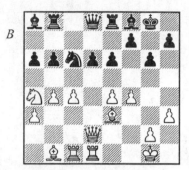

29 ...   b5?!

Vogt puts this down to time pressure in his *Informator* notes but it is already very hard to find a useful move for Black. For example after the natural **29...♛c7?!**, Black is embarrassed by 30 b5, winning a pawn.

The attempt to force the b6-pawn to b5 fails, so Black should try **29...♘h6** 30 ♘xb6 e5 31 ♘d5 ♘d4 with counterplay against the f4-pawn.

30	cxb5	axb5
31	♘c3	♘e7
32	♛e2!	

The correct plan. After 32 ♛xd6?! ♛xd6 33 ♖xd6 ♘d5 34 ♘xd5 exd5 35 ♖d7 dxe4 36 ♖cc7 ♖bc8, Black is very much alive.

32	...	♗c6
33	♗c5	♘c8
34	e5	♛c7

34...d5 35 ♗xf8 ♖xf8 36 ♘e4! with the idea of ♘f6+ is crushing for White.

35	exd6	♘xd6

Black would have preferred to play **35...♗xd6?** but it loses to 36 ♘e4 ♗xc5+ 37 ♖xc5 when he cannot stop a double attack on c6 and ♘f6+.

36	♛e5!	♖bd8
37	♗d4	f6

Losing a pawn but forced as Black must stop checkmate.

38	♛xf6	♗g7
39	♛xg7+	♛xg7
40	♗xg7	♔xg7
41	♗a2	♘f5?!

The beginning of a false plan. Though Black is a clear pawn down, White still has a lot of work to do and hence **41...♔f6** would have held out longer.

42	♔f2	

42 ♖xd8?! ♖xd8 43 ♗xe6 ♖d2 is unnecessary when White can easily win the position with his extra pawn.

42	...	♘d4
43	♗d5!	

With a bad bishop and a pawn less, Black cannot hope to hang on.

43	...	♗xd5
44	♖xd4	♗c4
45	♖cd1	♖xd4
46	♖xd4	g5 *(D)*

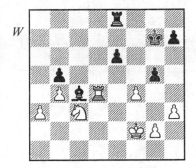

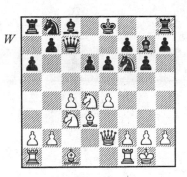

47	a4

47 fxg5 is equally good.

47	...	gxf4
48	axb5	&b3
49	&xf4	&c8
50	&g4+	&f8
51	&e4	&b8?
52	&c5	1-0

Analysis based on Vogt's notes in *Informator 58.*

An impressive victory by White, though the next game shows that with accurate and timely defence, Black's position is quite stubborn.

Game 13
Grünfeld-Psakhis
Tel-Aviv 1991

1 e4 c5 2 &f3 e6 3 d4 cxd4 4 &xd4 a6 5 &d3 &f6 6 0-0 &c7 7 &e2 d6 8 c4 g6 9 &c3 &g7 *(D)*

White foregoes the option of playing his bishop to f4 and instead opts for a more traditional set-up against the Hedgehog.

10	&e3?!	&bd7

Or 10...0-0 11 &ac1 &bd7 (11...b6 12 &fd1 &b7 13 f3 &bd7 14 &d2 &ac8 15 &f1 &fd8 16 &g5 &b8 with an edge for White was Agnos-Mortazavi, London Café Baroque 1994) and now:

a) 12 &b1 b6 13 &fd1 &b7 14 f3 &ac8 15 b3 &b8 16 &f2 &fe8 17 &de2 &a8 18 &d3 &e5 and though White again has a slight advantage, Black is poised to break out; Adams-Lobron, Brussels SWIFT 1992.

b) 12 &fd1 b6 13 f3 &b7 14 &f2 &ac8 15 &f1 &b8 16 b4 &fe8 17 &b3 &f8 18 a3 d5 19 cxd5 exd5 20 &xd5 &xd5 21 &xc8 &xc8 22 exd5 &d6 23 &h4 &c3 24 &d3 &xd3 25 &xd3 &xd5 26 &d2 b5 = Geller-Eingorn, Moscow 1986.

11	f4	0-0
12	&ac1	b6
13	&h1	&b7
14	b4 *(D)*	

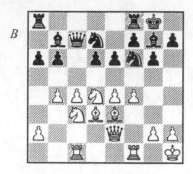

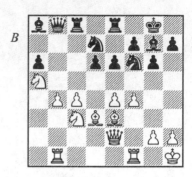

14 ...   Ife8!

A typical Hedgehog ploy. Black lines up his rook to the white queen on e2, hoping one day to open this file up with ...d5, exd5 exd5.

15 ♘b3   Iac8

16 a4

White correctly does not wait unnecessarily as Black is already well-placed for the ...d5 break. It is imperative that White diverts Black from playing this break by playing as quickly as possible on the queenside, as in the game.

16 ...   ♕b8

17 a5!?   bxa5

18 ♘xa5   ♗a8

19 Ib1 *(D)*   **♘h5**

The immediate **19...d5** is good in all cases apart from 20 e5!, which would give White a clear advantage.

20 ♕d2   ♕c7!

Steering clear of possible indirect attacks from the rook on b1 and at the same time keeping an eye on the knight on a5, thereby preventing the b4-b5 break.

21 Ibd1   Ib8

22 ♘a4   f5! *(D)*

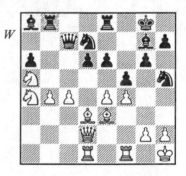

Played at exactly the right moment, when White has released some of his pressure on the d5-square. Now after **23 exf5**, Black can safely play 23...exf5, and d5 is compensated for by White's weakness on e4 – then 24 ♗e2

②hf6 25 ♗f3 ♗xf3 26 ♗xf3
♖xf3 27 ②e4 is ∓.

Suddenly, White's activity on
the queenside is meaningless and
the knights on a4 and a5 are offside.

23 c5

White has no choice but to
complicate in a difficult position.

23	...	dxc5
24	②xc5	②xc5
25	♗xc5	fxe4
26	♗e2	♖bd8
27	♕e3	♖xd1
28	♗xd1 (D)	

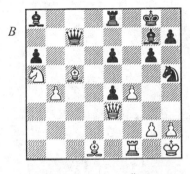

28 ...   ②f6!

Queens are bad blockaders of
passed pawns and this knight retreat ensures that the opening of
the a8-h1 diagonal will not be
long coming.

29 ♗a4   ②d5?!

29...♖d8 30 ♗b6 ②d5! 31
♗xc7 ②xe3 32 ♗xd8 ②xf1 with
good winning chances.

30 ♕e1   ♖c8

31	♕xe4	♕f7
32	♗b3	♗c3
33	♗d4?	♗xd4
34	♕xd4	②xf4

and White resigned as he has no
way to cover g2.

0-1

In all cases so far, Black has
opted to fianchetto the dark-
squared bishop rather than simply placing it on e7. The
following game (and the history
behind it) is the main reason for
this as White crushed Black on
every occasion the two players
met and the bishop went to e7.

Game 14
Nunn-Gheorghiu
Biel 1983

**1 e4 c5 2 ②f3 e6 3 d4 cxd4 4
②xd4 a6 5 ♗d3 ②f6 6 0-0 (D)**

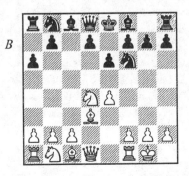

6 ...   d6

A surprisingly common move, which seems to me to be a bad one! There is no need for Black to commit himself so early, and 6...♕c7 is now considered the main line.

7 c4 *(D)*

Now White can afford to play this move as Black no longer has the option of playing 7...♘c6 and recapturing with his d-pawn.

Gheorghiu's first encounter with this line against John Nunn was in London in 1980 when Nunn had instead played 5 c4 ♘f6 6 ♘c3 d6 7 ♗e2. Nunn's treatment was nonetheless severe and the game continued 7...♗e7 8 0-0 0-0 9 f4 ♕c7 10 ♗e3 ♖e8 11 ♕e1 ♗f8 12 ♕h4 b6 13 ♖ae1 ♘bd7 14 ♗d3 ♗b7 15 ♗c2 g6 16 e5 ♘h5 17 exd6 ♗xd6 18 f5 ♘e5 19 fxe6 fxe6 20 ♘e4 ♘xc4 21 ♘xd6 ♕xd6 22 ♗h6 e5 23 ♘f5 ♕d5 24 ♖f2 ♕c5 25 ♗d1 ♗c8 26 b4 ♕xb4 27 ♘e7+ ♔h8 28 ♖ef1

♗e6 29 ♗xh5 ♕xe7 30 ♖f8+ ♕xf8 31 ♗xf8 ♖xf8 32 ♖xf8+ ♖xf8 33 ♕e7 ♖f4 34 g3 1-0.

7 ... b6

In fact, the only time in four encounters that Gheorghiu got any change from Nunn was in Vienna 1986 when he played something resembling the modern main line: **7...g6** 8 ♘c3 ♗g7 9 ♘b3 0-0 10 ♗e2 ♘c6 11 ♗f4 ♘e8 12 ♕d2 b6 13 ♖fd1 ♘e5 14 ♖ac1 ♕c7 15 ♗h6 ♗xh6 16 ♕xh6 ♗b7 17 ♘d4 ♘f6 18 ♕h4 ♕e7 19 f4 ♘c6 20 ♘xc6 ♗xc6 21 ♖d3 b5 22 e5 dxe5 23 fxe5 ♘d5 24 ♕xe7 ♘xe7 25 cxb5 axb5 26 ♖d4 ♘d5 27 ♘e4 ♘e7 28 ♘c3 ♘d5 29 a3 ♖fc8 30 ♘e4 ♗e8 31 ♖xc8 ♖xc8 32 ♘d6 ♖c1+ 33 ♖d1 ♘f4 34 ♗f3 ♖xd1+ 35 ♗xd1 ♗c6 36 ♗f3 ♗xf3 37 gxf3 ♘d3 38 b4 ♘xe5 39 ♔f2 g5 40 ♘xb5 f5 41 ♘d4 ♔f7 42 b5 ♘c4 43 a4 ♔e7 44 ♘b3 ♔d6 45 a5 e5 46 ♔e2 ♔d5 47 ♔d3 ½-½.

8 ♘c3 ♗b7

9 f4!

Black's early committal of his minor pieces gave White the option of playing more aggressively. White does not waste any time and goes straight for a king-side attack.

9 ... ♗e7

10 ♔h1 0-0

11 ♕e2 ♘c6

12 &xc6   &xc6 *(D)*

13 b3   &c7

The penultimate of the four epic Nunn-Gheorghiu encounters in Hamburg 1984 saw **13...&d7** 14 &b2 g6 15 &ad1 &e8 16 &b1 &c7 17 &d3 &f8 18 &b5 &xb5 19 cxb5 axb5 20 &xb5 &b7 21 &e2 b5 22 b4 &a6 23 &f3 &g7 24 &xg7 &xg7 25 &fd3 &c7 26 &h3 &b6 27 &d2 &f6 28 f5 exf5 29 exf5 d5 30 fxg6 fxg6 31 &f1 &g4 32 &d4+ &f6 33 &d3 h5 34 &xf6 &xf6 35 &f3 &e1+ 36 &f1 &e7 37 &g1 &e4 38 &c3 d4 39 &d3 &g4 40 h3 1-0.

Thus in 1980, Nunn crushed Gheorghiu by playing the slightly inaccurate version with &e2 (the bishop is better placed on d3). In 1983, the current game took place (a crushing win for White). In 1984, Gheorghiu 'improved' with 13...&d7 but still got no change. Finally, in 1986, Gheorghiu played the currently

recommended ...g6 against the Maroczy Bind and held Nunn to a draw. The reader can thus appreciate why this form of defence is currently very rarely seen!

Even in 1986, however, Gheorghiu played ...d6 far too early and White was given a free hand in the opening stage.

14 &b2   &ad8
15 &ae1   &b7
16 &b1 *(D)*

White has built up a menacing attacking formation. The two bishops on b2 and b1 are aimed at the black king, the rook on f1 can transfer to the kingside via f3 and either of the pawn breaks, f5 or e5, at an opportune moment is likely to cause havoc.

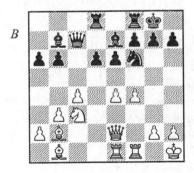

16 ...   &d7?!

Black simply does not have enough time to remove this vital defender from the kingside. However, the position is already very difficult and the suggested alternative of **16...g6** is hardly appetizing.

As Griffiths and Nunn point out in *Secrets of Grandmaster Play*, 16...g6 does however stand up well to a direct attack from White: 17 f5?! exf5 18 exf5 ♖de8 19 fxg6 hxg6 20 ♕f2 ♕c6 and Black's previously passive pieces have been activated by White's hasty play.

17 ♕h5!

An improvement over a previous game of Tringov's, which went **17 e5?** dxe5 18 fxe5 g6 when White's pawn on e5 is more of a liability than an asset.

17 ...   ♖fe8

An unpleasant move to have to make, but played more out of necessity than for a positive reason. When White places his f-pawn on f4 rather than the more traditional f3 in the Hedgehog (indeed, in any Sicilian), Black should be reluctant to move his rook from f8 to e8. The reasons for this are clearly shown in the game but in addition, by playing this rook move, Black leaves only his king defending the vulnerable f7-pawn and little protection of the f-file in general. Hence after f4-f5 and an exchange on either e6 or g6, White can often sacrifice a rook on either f7 or anywhere along the f-file.

A good example of this was seen in the game Sherzer-Olafsson, Philadelphia 1990. After 11...♖d8?!, White capitalized on Black's lack control along the f-file in spectacular fashion: 1 e4 c5 2 ♘f3 d6 3 d4 cxd4 4 ♘xd4 ♘f6 5 ♘c3 a6 6 ♗e3 e6 7 a4 ♘c6 8 ♗e2 ♗e7 9 0-0 0-0 10 f4 ♕c7 11 ♔h1 ♖d8 12 ♕e1 ♗d7 13 ♕g3 ♗f8 14 ♖ad1 ♖ac8 15 ♘f3 ♘b4 16 ♗d4 ♘e8 17 ♘g5! h6 18 ♗h5! hxg5 19 fxg5 g6 20 ♗xg6!! fxg6 21 ♖xf8+! ♔xf8 22 ♕f3+ ♔g8 23 ♖f1 ♘f6 24 ♕xf6 e5 25 ♕xg6+ 1-0.

18 ♖e3   ♘f6

The knight is forced humbly to return and protect the king.

19 ♕h3   g6

20 f5!

Now is the right time since Black has very little in the way of defence.

20 ...   ♗c8

After **20...exf5** 21 exf5!, Black is again in the same predicament and can make no use of the open a8-h1 diagonal.

21 ♖g3!

A fine move which retains maximum flexibility. There is no need to release the tension by exchanging the f5-pawn. At worst, it gives Black more to think about.

21 ...   ♔g7

22 ♕h4 *(D)*

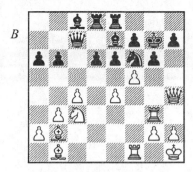

B

| 22 | ... | ♖f8 |

Black admits his mistakes and returns his rook to its best square. However, it is obviously too late as White has gained quite a few tempi for his attack.

23	♗c1!	♖de8
24	e5	dxe5
25	♕h6+	♔h8
26	♖h3	♖g8
27	♗g5	♖g7 *(D)*

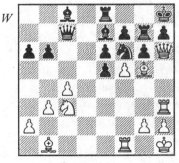

W

| 28 | ♗xf6 |

Nunn points out another way to win via **28 fxg6 ♕d8 29 ♗xf6 ♗xf6 30 ♕xh7+ ♖xh7 31 ♖xh7+ ♔g8 32 gxf7+ ♔f8 33 fxe8♕ ♔xe8 34 ♗g6+ ♔f8 35 ♖h8+.**

28	...	♗xf6
29	♘e4	♕d8
30	fxg6	♗e7
31	♕xh7+!	♖xh7
32	♖xh7+	♔g8
33	gxf7+	♔xh7
34	fxe8♕	1-0

In normal circumstances, I would have excluded the following section and merely mentioned it in a small note as being fine for Black. However, due to the surprising popularity of the system, I feel that a simple note is not enough to convince the reader and the white player!

7 c4 ♘c6!

Game 15
Murey-Psakhis
Tel-Aviv 1991

1 e4 c5 2 ♘f3 e6 3 d4 cxd4 4 ♘xd4 a6 5 ♗d3 ♘f6 6 0-0 ♕c7 7 c4?!

It is surprising how many people employ this line, which gives Black immediate equality. However, I suppose it is not altogether a shock as the majority of opening books do not even criticise the move. Even the Sicilian basher's bible, *Beating the Sicilian 2* by John Nunn only gives a fleeting mention of Black's possibilities. (*Editor's note:* but *Beating the Sicilian 3* advises White to avoid the line.)

Of course, Black can simply transpose to the main line with 7...d6 or 7...♗e7, but he has a better move at his disposal, which takes advantage of White's slightly artificial set-up in the centre.

7 ...   ♘c6!

One of the few occasions in the Kan when I consider it a viable option for Black to employ his knight on c6.

8 ♘xc6 (D)

White now has no viable option but to capture the knight on c6. Other moves such as 8 ♗e3 (or 8 ♘b3) allow 8...♘e5! with the dual threats of ...♘xc4 and ...♘eg4, attacking h2 and e3. 8 ♘f3 transposes to game 17, Kamsky-I.Gurevich.

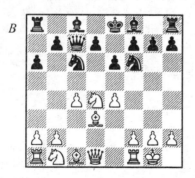

8 ...   dxc6

8...bxc6 is playable, but why pass upon a clear equalising line that also gives excellent winning chances?

9 f4

The only way to try to justify his 7th move. Other moves have been played but there is no doubting Black's easy development, e.g. **9 ♘c3 e5 10 h3** and now:

a) **10...♗c5 11 ♗g5 ♗e6 12 ♖c1 ♕e7 13 ♕f3 ♖d8 14 ♖fd1 ♗d4 =** as in Jönsson-Eingorn, Reykjavik 1989.

b) **10...♘d7 11 ♕f3 ♘c5 12 ♗c2 ♘e6 13 ♘e2 ♗c5 14 ♗e3 a5 15 ♖ad1 0-0 16 ♗xc5 ♘xc5 17 ♕e3 ♘e6 18 f4? exf4 19 ♘xf4 ♘xf4 20 ♖xf4 ♕e5 21 b3 ♗e6 ∓** Rimawi-Gheorghiu, Thessaloniki OL 1988.

9 ...   e5!

The point of Black's early knight move. 9...e5! suddenly highlights a big weakness on d4 in White's camp and at the same time liberates the bishop on c8.

Note that after **10 fxe5?**, Black does not immediately recapture with **10...♕xe5**, when 11 ♗f4 wins White a useful tempo, but instead plays **10...♘g4!**, when White's position is suddenly hopeless.

Apart from the huge positional drawbacks in White's position in the shape of the isolated e-pawn,

White also has tactical problems on the dark squares.

10 f5 *(D)*

This is probably the only move. 10 ♔h1?! has been played but in my opinion Black can drum up quite an initiative by following the same plan as in the game continuation, viz. **10...♗c5**:

a) 11 ♘c3 ♘g4 12 ♕f3 ♕d8!! as in Morris-Mortazavi, London Café Baroque 1994.

b) 11 ♕f3 ♗g4 12 ♕g3 ♕d7 13 h3 0-0-0 14 ♗c2 ♘h5 15 ♕h4 ♗c2 16 ♖e1 exf4 17 ♗xf4 ♘xf4 18 ♕xf4 ♗xc4 19 ♘c3 ♕d2! was a quick victory for Black in Schlosser-Vyzhmanavin, Hungary 1989.

From the above diagram it is clear that White has a far from ideal position, both positionally and tactically.

Positionally, his bishop on d3 is hemmed in by his own pawns on c4, e4 and f5. In addition the d4-square is woefully weak and White has no way in which to repair his damaged structure. Tactically, the white king will be harassed along the a7-g1 diagonal.

The only possible justification for playing this line is the spatial advantage that White can boast due to his still intact Maroczy Bind. However, this game shows that Black can continually harass White before this spatial advantage can be realised.

Note that a very similar position to the previous diagram can be reached via a different move order:

1 e4 c5 2 ♘f3 e6 3 d4 cxd4 4 ♘xd4 a6 5 ♘c3 ♕c7 6 ♗d3 ♘f6 7 0-0 ♘c6 8 ♘xc6 dxc6 9 f4 e5 10 f5 *(D)*

However, the absence of the white pawn from c4 has a huge consequence on the evaluation of the position. It is not enough for

Black simply to concentrate on his kingside attack, as this attack on its own is defensible. As is so often the case in chess, a combination of positional and tactical ideas is needed to maintain the dynamic balance.

| 10 | ... | ♗c5+ |
| 11 | ♔h1 | h5!? |

There is no doubt that this is an ambitious plan, but nevertheless a plan I would highly recommend if Black is playing all-out for a win.

Black can also simply play on White's weakness on d4: **11...h6** 12 ♘c3 ♗d4 13 ♗d2 b6 14 ♖b1 ♗b7 15 b4 ♖d8 16 ♕e2 0-0 was Agnos-Bischoff, Bad Wörishofen 1993, with roughly equal chances.

| 12 | ♘c3 | ♘g4 |
| 13 | ♕f3 *(D)* | |

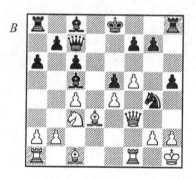

| 13 | ... | ♕d8! |

A highly unusual concept so early in the game. The black queen seemingly 'undevelops' but sets up the annoying threat of ...♕h4 and ...♘f2+.

14 ♘d1

14 h3? ♘f2+! nets Black the exchange. Another possibility here was **14 ♗e2** ♕h4 15 h3 ♘f2+ 16 ♔h2 ♘g4+ when Black has at least a draw but can still play the position on if necessary.

| 14 | ... | ♕h4 |
| 15 | ♕h3? | |

A mistake by White which simply gives him a bad endgame. For an alternative, see the next game McDonald-Emms.

As a general rule, if Black can manage to develop his problematic queen's bishop and castle safely, White will find it hard to parry the tactical and positional threats.

15	...	♕xh3
16	gxh3	♘f6∓
17	♘c3	b5

17...b6 is equally viable since White cannot disrupt Black's development sufficiently, e.g. 18 ♘a4 ♗d4 19 c5?! b5! (but not 19...bxc5 when White has at least managed to hem in the light-squared bishop on c8) 20 ♘b6 ♖b8 and White cannot avoid losing a pawn.

18	♗g5	♗d4
19	cxb5	axb5
20	♖ac1	♗b7! *(D)*

There is no need to rush the win with **20...b4?!** since White can cause trouble after 21 ♘e2 ♗xb2 22 ♖c2 ♗a3 23 ♖c5!. It is important to note that Black's positional advantage is long-term and hence the win is not going to 'run away'.

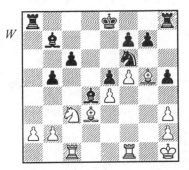

| 21 | a3 | 0-0-0! |
| 22 | ♘d5?! | |

A typical mistake by the side that has been under pressure since the early opening. White's position is of course dismal but Black should still need to show his technique. Instead **22 ♔g2!** would have forced Black to work hard. The text move, however, forces a strong continuation.

| 22 | ... | ♘xd5 |

Not **22...♖xd5?** 23 ♗xf6! (not 23 exd5 when 23...c5! unleashes the bishop on b7) and Black has lost his grip.

| 23 | ♗xd8 | ♘f4 |
| 24 | ♖xf4 | exf4 |

25	♗g5	f3!
26	♖f1	♗xb2
27	♖xf3	c5∓

The rest of the game is self-explanatory.

28 ♔g2 c4 29 ♗c2 ♖e8 30 ♔f1 ♗xe4 31 ♖e3 ♗c6 32 ♖xe8+ ♗xe8 33 ♗e7 ♗c6 34 h4 ♔d7 35 ♗f8 ♗e5 36 ♗d1 ♗e4 0-1

Game 16
McDonald-Emms
British Ch (Norwich) 1994

1 e4 c5 2 ♘f3 e6 3 d4 cxd4 4 ♘xd4 a6 5 ♗d3 ♘f6 6 0-0 ♕c7 7 c4 ♘c6 8 ♘xc6 dxc6 9 f4 e5 10 f5 ♗c5+ 11 ♔h1 h5 12 ♘c3 ♘g4 13 ♕f3 ♕d8! 14 ♘d1 ♕h4 (D)

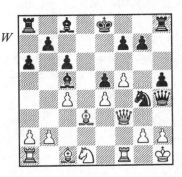

| 15 | h3 | |

15 ♕h3?! was Murey-Psakhis – see previous annotated game.

| 15 | ... | b6 |

Black can expand further with **15...b5?!**, but he pays for this by seriously weakening his pawn structure. In addition, after ...b5, the b-pawn is on a light square and this can only further hinder the troublesome bishop on c8.

15...b6 also has the idea of playing ...♗b4 and ...c5.

16	♗d2	♗b7
17	b4	♗d4 (D)

18 ♖b1

After **18 ♗c3, 18...0-0-0?** 19 c5 was a game Emms-Agnos, with a clear advantage to White. Instead, **18...c5!** would have been enough for equality.

18	...	c5

This move is forced as White was himself threatening to play the pawn sacrifice c5 when the open lines would be enough compensation for the pawn.

19	bxc5	♗xc5
20	♗b4	♗d4
21	c5?	

Too ambitious. White should have taken the draw on offer with 21 ♗c3 when Black has nothing

better than to repeat with ...♗c5, with a draw.

21	...	bxc5
22	♗xc5	♗xc5
23	♖xb7	0-0! ∓

A good example of how late castling can dramatically turn a position. Black has got rid of his 'problem piece' in this line, the bishop on b7, and is now ready to make use of the open d-file.

24 ♘c3?!

White's last chance was simply to block Black's infiltration down the d-file with **24 ♗c4!** followed by ♗d5.

24	...	♘f2+!
25	♔h2	♖ad8!
26	♗xa6 (D)	

Now **26 ♘d5?** is no longer possible due to 26...♖xd5! 27 exd5 e4!, winning.

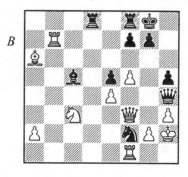

26	...	♖d2!

Another black piece enters the attack against the white king and the pressure on White's position is now too much.

27	♗e2	♘g4+
28	♔h1	♗d4
29	♖c7	♖b8!
30	f6	

A desperate sacrifice to divert Black's knight from g4, which Black rightly ignores.

30	...	g6!
31	♗c4	♖f2
32	♕d3	♖xf1+
33	♕xf1	♕g3

0-1

Game 17
Kamsky-I.Gurevich
New York 1991

1 e4 c5 2 ♘f3 e6 3 d4 cxd4 4 ♘xd4 a6

5 c4

This is one of White's other viable options to the Main Line. However, White has recently shown a preference for forcing Black to develop his king's bishop on g7 in the Hedgehog. One of the drawbacks of 5 c4 is that Black retains maximum flexibility over the development of all his pieces.

5	...	♘f6
6	♘c3	♕c7
7	♗d3	♘c6! *(D)*

We have now nearly transposed to the first annotated game

with the difference that White has played his knight to c3 instead of castling. Nevertheless, the same principles still apply as White has still indirectly weakened d4.

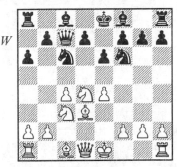

8 ♘f3?!

A dubious idea as White hinders the advance of his f-pawn for very little in return. The best move at this stage was probably **8 ♘xc6 dxc6 9 0-0**, with a direct transposition to Game 1.

8 ...   b6!

An excellent non-committal move which again retains maximum flexibility. **8...♗c5** is tempting, but White would then answer with **9 ♗g5!** when Black would either have to allow some damage to his pawn structure (♗xf6) or humbly retreat with his bishop to e7.

9 0-0   ♘g4!

After this move, it is easy to understand why White prefers the main line to the early c4 option. In the main line of the Kan,

1 e4 c5 2 ♘f3 e6 3 d4 cxd4 4 ♘xd4 a6 5 ♗d3 ♕c7 6 0-0 ♘f6 7 ♕e2 d6, White has forced Black to play ...d6, thereby closing the b8-h2 diagonal. This game shows that as well as maintaining flexibility by delaying ...d6, Black also has very substantial threats along this diagonal.

10 h3?!

It is imperative for White to force Black to play ...d6 as quickly as possible. Hence the immediate **10 g3** is preferable to the text. However, that is not to say that Black is without a plan. After 10...h5 11 ♗f4 d6! (11...♗d6?! 12 ♗xd6 ♕xd6 13 ♗e2 and White has regrouped) Black will develop in normal Sicilian fashion with equal chances for both sides.

10 ...   h5 (D)

The thematic plan. Note that after **11 hxg4**, Black does not immediately checkmate White

(11...hxg4 12 g3 gxf3 13 ♕xf3), but the open h-file will guarantee dangerous play.

11 g3

With this move, White puts a stop to all of Black's mating ideas. However, it is essential to understand that the mating threats were never dangerous on their own. Black has merely used some tactical themes to develop with tempo and at the same time, by forcing White to move his pawns, seriously weaken White's structure.

11 ...   ♘ge5
12 ♗e3 (D)

12 ...   h4!

An enormously powerful move which in one stroke highlights White's artificial set-up.

13 g4

After 13 ♘xh4, not 13...♖xh4? which leads to nothing, but the simple 13...♘xd3! 14 ♕xd3 ♘e5 and Black will at least regain the sacrificed pawn by capturing on c4.

13 ...   ♗d6!!

The double exclamation mark is perhaps a little excessive, but Black has skilfully managed to set up the ideal Sicilian Kan. In many respects, the king's bishop naturally belongs on d6 but in the majority of positions White will force ...d6 by threatening f4 and e5. Occasionally, Black gets away with this but then has serious problems with his light-squared bishop as the d-pawn is hindered.

In the above diagram, however, each Black minor piece is ideally placed to capitalise on White's weaknesses.

Of course, the main justification for placing the bishop on d6 in this position is to overprotect the vulnerable f4-square.

14 ♖c1

A more natural plan would have been **14 ♘xe5 ♘xe5 15 f4** in an attempt to 'repair' f4. Black, however, has a number of good options, one of them being the simple **15...♗c5! 16 ♕d2 ♗xe3+ 17 ♕xe3 ♘xd3 18 ♕xd3 ♗b7** when White is badly overstretched and has the disadvantage of knight v bishop. Nevertheless, this is a far better option than the plan in the game.

14 ...   ♘xf3+
15 ♕xf3   ♘e5
16 ♕d1 *(D)*

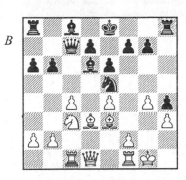

16 ...   ♘g6

A complete triumph. Black is simply 'attacking' f4 three times compared to White's lonely bishop on e3.

17 ♖e1

This allows Black a free hand. It would have been better to slightly disrupt his plans with **17 c5!? bxc5 18 ♘a4 ♘f4** when Black's advantage is undoubted, but at least White has eradicated the black knight.

17 ...   ♗h2+!

Forcing the king to an awkward square.

18 ♔h1   ♗f4
19 ♗f1   ♗xe3
20 ♖xe3 *(D)* **0-0?**

The diagram below is one of the rare cases when the king belongs in the centre as it can then defend Black's weakness on d6.

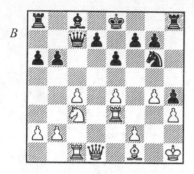

Best would have been **20...Rb8!** when after 21 Wd4 f6 22 Rd1 Ne5 23 Na4 Wc6!, Black would then follow up with ...Ke7 and ...g5, with an impregnable set-up.

21	Wd4	Wf4?
22	Kg1	Rb8
23	Rd1	Rd8
24	Bg2	f6
25	Na4	b5
26	Nc5	Bb7
27	Nxb7?	

A serious error as White exchanges the only possible 'defender' of the f4-square, leaving himself with a bad bishop v good knight. Considerably better was **27 cxb5** axb5 28 Nd3 Wc7 29 Rc1 when Black's grip on f4 has been nullified.

27	...	Rxb7
28	cxb5	axb5
29	Rb3	Rbb8
30	Wd2	Kf7
31	Wa5	We5

32 Rbd3 (D)

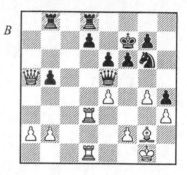

32	...	Ke8!

Finally, Black finds the correct plan of using the king as a useful defensive piece.

33	Wd2	Wc7
34	Rd6?!	Ne5
35	b3	g5!

The final piece in the jigsaw. Black's dark-square domination is complete and White is hopelessly passive.

36 Rc1 Wa7 37 Kh1 Rbc8 38 Rd1 Wc7 39 Bf1 Wc3 40 We2? b4 41 Bg2 Ke7 42 R6d4 Rb8 43 R4d2 Rdc8 44 Wf1 Rc7 45 f4? Ng6 46 fxg5 fxg5 47 Rf2 Ne5!∓ 48 Wa6 Rc6 49 We2 Rcc8 + 50 Wa6 Rc6 51 We2 Rcc8 52 Wa6 Wc5 53 We2 Rf8 54 Rxf8 Rxf8 55 Wd2 Rf4 56 a3?! bxa3 57 b4 Wb5! 58 Wc3 a2 59 Ra1 Rf2 60 Wd4 Rc2 61 Bf1 Wb8 62 Bg2 Wd6 63 Wg1 Wd2 64 b5 Nd3 65 Wf1 Rc1 0-1

4 Scheveningen-type systems

The Scheveningen systems are possibly the hardest to come to grips with in the Kan. The number of possible transpositions to other systems, such as the Taimanov and the Scheveningen itself, makes it an extremely difficult line to master.

The earliest opportunity that White can adopt the more classical Sicilian approach (as opposed to the Hedgehog systems) is on move 5 after the moves 1 e4 c5 2 ♘f3 e6 3 d4 cxd4 4 ♘xd4 a6: 5 ♘c3 (D)

Perhaps this is not the most flexible approach and therefore I shall consider the position after 5 ♗d3 ♘f6 6 0-0 ♕c7 7 ♘c3 as the main line. After this position has

been dealt with, the end of this chapter shall contain some games where White plays 5 ♘c3.

Some of Black's options have been outlined in Chapter 2, and if White wishes to play a system with ♘c3 and ♗d3, then the following position will invariably be reached:

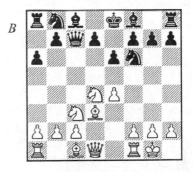

And here, Black has two main moves (and other lesser moves which shall be discussed within the annotated games): 7...♗c5!?, a relatively new system; and the older 7...♘c6, which is 'halfway' between a Taimanov and a Kan.

I purposely describe 7...♘c6 as 'halfway' between a Taimanov Sicilian and a Kan as there is now a real ambiguity over what signifies a Kan and a Taimanov. It is interesting that in *Winning with the Sicilian*, Taimanov groups the systems with 7...♘c6 under the Kan Variation of the Sicilian. In the final chapter of his book, according to my own formula, he equates the Taimanov to when Black places his king's knight on e7 and plays ...♘c6xd4 followed by ...♘e7-c6. In practice, however, there is no such consensus. Indeed, one well-known grandmaster once asked me why I play the Kan when the Taimanov was 'better'. On further investigation, we both seemed to play the same thing, the only difference being that he plays 1 e4 c5 2 ♘f3 e6 3 d4 cxd4 4 ♘xd4 ♘c6, allowing 5 ♘b5, whereas I play 4...a6.

The following section concentrates on the current 'main line' with 7...♗c5. Discussion of the other popular line, 7...♘c6, follows the 7.....♗c5 section.

Black plays 7...♗c5

Game 18
Tischbierek-Bischoff
Hannover IBM 1991

1 e4 c5 2 ♘f3 e6 3 d4 cxd4 4 ♘xd4 a6 5 ♘c3 ♕c7 6 ♗d3 ♘f6 7 0-0 *(D)*

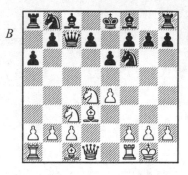

7 ...   ♗c5

a) **7...d6?!** has been played but as in all the other examples in this book of a premature ...d6, it is inflexible. 7...d6?! does nothing to solve the problem of the active knight on d4 (see Chapter 2) and should be avoided for the more active options available to Black.

However, White does seem to let Black get away with this move by simply playing down known lines instead of attempting to punish Black for showing his cards too early.

a1) **8 ♗e3 ♘bd7 9 f4 b5 10 a3 ♗b7 11 ♕f3 ♗e7 12 ♕g3 g6 13 ♘f3 ♘c5 14 ♗d4 0-0 15 ♘g5 ♘h5 16 ♕g4 e5!** 17 fxe5 dxe5 18 ♗e3 ♖ad8 19 ♖ad1 ♘f4 20 ♗xf4 exf4 21 ♘h3 ♘e6 22 ♘xf4 ♘xf4 23 ♕xf4 ♗d6 24 ♕h4 ♗e7 25 ♕g4 ♗xa3! ∓ was Trkaljanov-Kovačević, Yugoslav Ch 1991.

a2) A more direct approach was seen in Wedberg-C.Ionescu, Berlin 1988 after **8 f4 ♗e7 9 ♘f3**

♘bd7 10 ♕e1 0-0 11 e5 ♘e8 12 ♕g3 ♘c5 13 ♗c3 ♗d7? (13... ♘xd4 14 cxd3 ∓) 14 ♗xh7+! ♔xh7 15 ♘g5+ ♔g8 16 ♕h4 ♗xg5 17 fxg5 ♗c6 18 ♖f4 dxe5 19 g6 fxg6 20 ♖xf8+ ♔xf8 21 ♕h8+ ♔e7 22 ♗xc5+ ♔d7 23 ♖f1 ♔c8 24 ♘e4 ♗d7 25 ♘d6+ ♔b8 26 b4 ♕c6 27 ♘xe8 ♗xe8 28 ♕xg7 b6 29 ♖f8 ♖a7 30 ♕g8 ♖d7 31 ♖xe8+ ♔a7 32 ♗e3 ♕e4 33 ♗xb6+ ♔xb6 34 ♕xe6+ ♔c7 35 ♕xe5+ 1-0.

a3) At the other end of the scale, White can go a little too far, as in Tischbierek-De Boer, Ostend 1991 which went **8 ♔h1 ♘c6 9 ♗e3 g6 10 f4 ♗g7 11 ♘f3 0-0 12 ♕e1 b5 13 ♕h4 ♖e8 14 e5 ♘d5 15 ♘xd5 exd5 16 f5!? gxf5 17 exd6 ♕xd6 18 ♗f4 ♕f6 19 ♗g5 ♕xb2 20 ♖ab1 ♕a3 21 ♗f6 ♕d6 22 ♗xg7 ♔xg7 23 ♘g5 h6 24 ♗xf5 ♘e5 25 ♘h3 ♘g6 26 ♕d4+ ♕e5 27 ♕d3 ♗xf5 28 ♖xf5 ♕e4 29 ♖bf1 ♖a7 30 ♕d1 ♖c7 31 c3 ♖e5 ∓** though White held eventually held the draw.

b) **7...♗e7?! 8 ♔h1** comes under the same bracket as 7...d6?!.

b1) Again, White often plays inaccurately as in Howell-Vasiukov, Belgorod 1990 which went **8...d6 9 f4 ♘bd7 10 ♘f3 0-0 11 ♕e2 ♘c5 12 ♗e3 b5 13 ♗d4 ♗b7 14 b4 ♘xd3 15 cxd3 ♗c6 16 ♕b2 ♕b7 17 ♘d2 a5! 18 a3 axb4 19** axb4 ♖xa1 20 ♖xa1 ♖a8 21 ♘b3 ♖xa1+ 22 ♕xa1 h6 23 ♕a7 ♕xa7 24 ♗xa7 d5! 25 ♘d4 ♗b7 26 e5 ♘h5 27 g3 ♗xb4 28 ♘cxb5 ♗a6 29 ♔g2 g6 30 ♔f3 ♘g7 31 ♔e2 ½-½.

b2) On the other hand, sometimes White does not hang around: **8...b5 9 f4 d6? 10 e5! ♘d5 11 ♘xd5 exd5 12 e6! ♗f6 13 exf7+ ♕xf7 14 ♖e1+ ♔f8 15 ♘f5 ♕c7 16 ♕h5 g6 17 ♕h6+ ♔f7 18 ♖e7+ ♗xe7 19 ♕g7+ ♔e6 20 ♗d2 ♖c8 21 ♖e1+ ♔d7 22 ♘xe7 ♔d8 23 f5 ♕xe7 24 ♖xe7 ♖xe7 25 ♗g5 ♖aa7 26 ♕f8+ 1-0** was a crushing victory in Lau-Lutz, Graz Z 1993.

The advantages of 7...♗c5 have been described in full in Chapter 2. The main idea behind the move is immediately to put a question to the knight on d4.

8 ♘b3 *(D)*

The main move. The only other alternative is **8 ♗e3**, which is discussed in the next game.

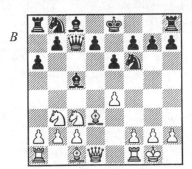

8 ...   **♗e7**

8...♗a7?! seems a reasonable enough move if White chooses the wrong option.

a) **9 ♕e2?!** d6 10 ♗e3? (the question mark is not for the strength of the move but for White falling to take advantage of 8...♗a7?!) 10...♗xe3 11 ♕xe3 b5 12 ♘e2 0-0 13 ♖ac1 ♘bd7 14 c4 bxc4 15 ♖xc4 ♕b8 16 ♗b1 a5 17 ♕d2 ♗a6 18 ♖c3 e5 19 ♖d1 a4 20 ♘bc1 ♘c5 21 ♘g3 ♖d8 22 ♘ce2 ♕b6 23 ♖cc1 ♖ab8 24 ♘c3 ♕xb2 25 ♕g5 ♘e6 26 ♕e3 a3 27 ♘f5 ♕b6 28 ♕g3 g6 29 ♕h4 ♘h5 30 ♘d5 ♕b2 31 g4 ♗e2 32 gxh5 gxf5 33 exf5 ♗xd1 34 ♖xd1 ♕e2 35 ♖c1 ♕d2 36 fxe6+ 0-1, a classical Sicilian win for Black in Klovans-Cu.Hansen, Groningen 1992.

b) The 'solution' can be found in a game played way back in 1973 between Radulov-Quinteros, Leningrad IZ, which went **9 ♗g5!** ♕e5 (in Howell-Cullip, British Ch 1990, Black allowed White to capture on f6 with 9...d6?! 10 ♗xf6 gxf6 11 ♕g4 ♘d7 12 ♕g7 ♖f8 13 ♕xh7 ♘e5 14 ♔h1 and Black could not claim much in the way of compensation) 10 ♕d2 ♘h5 11 ♔h1 h6 12 ♗e3 g5 13 ♘a4 ♕c7 14 c4 b6 15 ♗d4 e5 16 ♗e3 d6 17 ♖fd1 ♘f6 18 f3 ♘bd7 19 ♗f1 ♔e7 20 ♖ac1 ♗b7 21 ♘c3 ♘c5 22 ♘a1 ♖ad8 23 b4 ♘cd7 24 ♗f2 ♘f8 25 ♘c2 ♘g6 26 ♘e3 ±.

9 f4   **d6** *(D)*

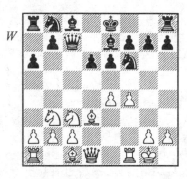

10 ♕f3

f3 seems to be the best square for the queen. White occasionally plays **10 ♕e2** but nearly always finds that the queen must be transferred to the kingside via f3 or e1 to either h3 or g3:

a) **10...♘c6** 11 ♔h1 0-0 12 ♗d2 b6 13 ♖ae1 ♗b7 14 a3 g6 15 ♖f3 ♖fe8 16 ♖h3 ♗f8 17 ♕f2 ♗g7 18 ♕h4 ♖f8 19 ♘e2 ♕d8 20 ♖f1 ♖c8 21 c3 h5 22 ♕e1 ♘g4 23 ♘g3 ♕e8 24 ♗c1 f5 25 ♘d2 b5?! and now had Black played 25 ...d5! in Schäfer-Chuchelov, Porz 1992, it would have been ∓.

b) One way to justify the positioning of the queen on e2 is to play g2-g4-g5 followed by ♕h5 in one go (rather than the queen having to go from e2-f3-g3 or h3). There has only been one practical example of this plan and Black came off better in Nagatz-Dautov, Bad Lauterberg 1991 after **10...♘bd7** 11 ♗d2 b5 12 a3 ♗b7 13 ♖ae1 0-0 14 g4 ♘c5 15 g5 ♘fd7 16 ♖f3 ♖fe8 17 ♖h3 ♘f8? (better was 17...g6 and ...♗f8-g7) 18 ♕g4 ♘xd3 19 cxd3 d5 20 f5 exf5 21 exf5 ♗d6 22 ♖f1 d4 23 ♘e4 ♗xe4 24 dxe4 ♕c2 25 ♖e1 d3 26 ♗c3 ♕xb3 27 ♗xg7 ♔xg7 28 f6+ ♔g8 29 ♕h5 d2 30 ♖d1 ♗c5+ 31 ♔h1 ♕c4 0-1.

10 ...   ♘bd7 (D)

10...♘c6?! was disastrous in Landenbergue-Martinović, Geneva 1992 after 11 ♗d2 0-0 12 ♖ae1 ♘b4? 13 e5 ♘xd3 14 cxd3 dxe5 15 fxe5 ♘d7 16 ♕g3 ♔h8 17 d4 ♘b6 18 ♗g5! ♗xg5 19 ♕xg5 ♗d7 20 ♖e3 ♕d8 21 ♕h5 ♗e8 22 ♖h3 h6 23 ♖f6!! 1-0. Black must be extremely careful about attempting to play a Scheveningen Sicilian when White's bishop is aggressively posted on d3.

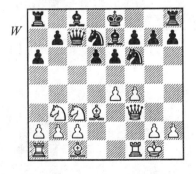

W

11 a4?!

In conjunction with 12 ♗d2 (see game continuation), I don't think that this move fits in with White's plan. The immediate **11 ♗d2** was seen in Akopian-Kamsky, Palma de Mallorca 1989 when Black did not play 11...b5 but **11...b6!**. The reason for this is that **11...b5?** would give White an advantage after 12 a4! b4 13 ♘a2! when Black would have to weaken b5 with 13...a5. A lot of players have made this mistake, Howell-Emms, Cappelle la Grande 1994 transposed to this position with 10 a4?! b6 11 ♕f3 ♘bd7 12 ♗d2 ♗b7 13 ♕g3 0-0 14 ♖ae1 and after 14...d5! 15 exd5 ♘xd5 16 ♘xd5 ♗xd5 17 ♕h3 f5 Black had a slight advantage.

With the correct 11...b6, Kamsky had the right idea but erred later: Akopian-Kamsky continued 12 ♕g3 g6? 13 e5 ♘h5 14 ♕f3 ♗b7 15 exd6 ♗xd6 16 ♗e4 0-0-0 17 ♗xb7+ ♕xb7 18 ♘e4 ♗e7 19 ♗c3 ♘hf6 20 ♖ae1 ♖hf8 21 ♗d4 ♘xe4 22 ♖xe4 ♕c6 23 ♕e2 ♔b8 24 ♖e3 ♘c5 25 ♖c3 ♕e4 26 ♗e5+ ♔a8 27 ♖e3 ♕b7 with an unclear position according to *Informator 50*, though I prefer White.

11 ...   b6
12 ♗d2   ♗b7

13	♖ae1	0-0	
14	♕h3	♖ad8 *(D)*	

15 g4?!

Mainka-Bischoff, Baden-Baden 1992 reached the above diagram as well but White instead continued **15 f5** though Black held comfortable after 15...exf5 16 ♘d5 ♘xd5 17 exd5 ♘e5 18 ♘d4 ♗f6 19 ♘xf5 ♘xd3 20 ♕xd3 ♕c5+ 21 ♗e3 ♕xd5 22 ♕xd5 ♗xd5 23 ♘h6+ gxh6 24 ♖xf6 ♖fe8 25 ♖xh6 b5 26 axb5 axb5 27 ♖h4 ♖e4 28 ♖xe4 ♗xe4 29 c3 f5 30 ♗d4 ♔f7 ½-½. I would say that the diagram position is equal and White needs to find an improvement in other variations.

15 ... d5!

A classical break in the centre to counteract a flank attack.

16	exd5	♗c5+!
17	♗e3	

17 ♘xc5 ♘xc5! gives Black the advantage after 18 g5 ♘xd3 19 cxd3 ♘xd5.

17	...	exd5
18	g5	♘e4!

The knight gives Black clear compensation for the loss of the bishop pair.

19	♘xc5	♘dxc5

19...bxc5!? is playable but after 20 ♘xe4 dxe4 21 ♗e2 White has at least managed to block the h1-a8 diagonal.

20	♗d4	♖fe8
21	♖e3	♗c8
22	f5	♕d6
23	♕h4 *(D)*	

The start of a faulty plan. White must stay as solid as possible and keep his blockade on d4 for as long as possible. The text fails to a tactical coup which gives Black a winning advantage.

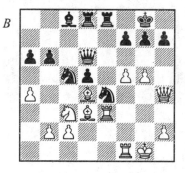

23	...	♘xd3
24	♖h3?	♗xf5!
25	♖xf5	♕g6
26	♖hf3	♘dc5
27	♔h1	♘e6!

Black temporarily sacrifices two pawns to remove the useful white bishop on d4 and open up lines for his rooks.

28	♗xb6	♖c8
29	♘xd5	♘6xg5
30	♖f1	♖xc2
31	♕f4	h6
32	♖g1 *(D)*	

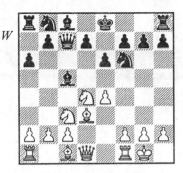

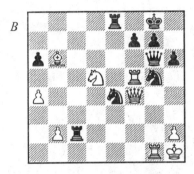

32 ... ♕c6!

Lining up the queen to the white king on h1, as White cannot possibly hold on to d5 for long.

33 ♖e5 ♖xe5 34 ♕xe5 ♘f6 35 ♖d1 ♖d2! 36 ♖xd2 ♕c1+ 37 ♔g2 ♕xd2+ 38 ♔g1 ♕xd5 39 ♕b8+ ♔h7 40 ♗e3 ♕f3 0-1

Game 19
Motwani-Bischoff
Groningen 1990

1 e4 c5 2 ♘f3 e6 3 d4 cxd4 4 ♘xd4 a6 5 ♘c3 ♕c7 6 ♗d3 ♘f6 7 0-0 ♗c5 *(D)*

8 ♗e3

A perfectly reasonable move though I am always glad when White adopts this possibility instead of 8 ♘b3. The drawback to this system is that White invariably has to move his knight on d4 and therefore exchange dark-squared bishops.

In many instances this favours Black. As one of Black's main ideas in these systems is to play ...e5, the following type of position can be avoided:

Here, Black has played the standard ...e5 idea but has been

left with a typical bad bishop which is hemmed in by his own pawns on d6 and e5. Thus we can see the reason why Black is happy when White volunteers to exchange dark-squared bishops.

The game continuation is a fine example of a 'good ...e5' when Black has got rid of his troublesome bishop on e7 and therefore has the advantage.

8	...	d6

8...b5? was seen in Ivanchuk-J.Polgar, Monaco Amber rpd 1994 when White came crashing through after 9 ♘dxb5! axb5 10 ♘xb5 ♕e5 11 ♗xc5 ♕xc5 12 b4! ♕b6 13 e5 ♘d5 14 ♘d6+ ♔e7 15 ♕h5 g6 16 ♗xg6 ♘c6 17 ♗e4 ♔d8 18 b5 ♘ce7 19 c4 ♘f4 20 ♕f3 ♘xg2 21 ♗xa8 ♘h4 22 ♕f6 ♖g8+ 23 ♔h1 ♘hf5 24 ♘xf5 ♗b7+ 25 f3 ♗xa8 26 ♘xe7 1-0.

9	♕e2	♘bd7
10	a4 *(D)*	

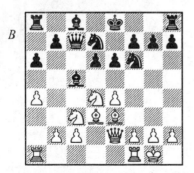

10	...	b6

Black voluntarily gives his dark-squared bishop no retreat squares, correctly assessing that it will be exchanged for its white counterpart anyway.

11 ♘b3?!

It would have been better to delay this for as long as possible with 11 f4 and ♔h1 though Black has enough time to organise a proper defence.

11	...	♗xe3
12	♕xe3	0-0
13	♖ae1	♗b7
14	♕g3	♖fe8
15	f4 *(D)*	

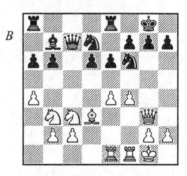

15	...	e5!

The perfect example of the ...e5 break. Black has a 2:1 protection over d5 and he has got rid of his dark-squared bishop. We can therefore safely say that Black has a small positional advantage.

16	f5	♘c5!

The immediate 16...d5? would have been premature after 17

exd5 ♘xd5 18 ♘e4! ♘df6 19 ♘bd2! and White has the advantage due to his blockade of e4.

17 ♖e3

After **17 ♘xc5?!** ♕xc5+ 18 ♔h1 b5! followed by ...b4 Black has complete control of d5.

17 ... ♖ad8!

A good ploy by Black and one which is adopted by all top players. Of course Black can play 17...d5 immediately but in practice, execution of a threat is often a worse option than retaining it. Apart from the psychological factor of retaining the tension in the position, 17...♖ad8 also 'overprotects' d5, a ploy recommended by the great chess strategist, Nimzowitsch.

18 ♕h4 h6
19 ♖g3 *(D)*

19 ... ♔f8!

A fine move which prepares the king for the endgame and sidesteps any of White's tactical ideas.

20 ♖ff3 ♕e7
21 ♖h3 *(D)*

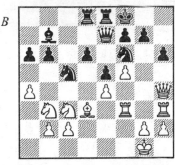

21 ... d5!∓

With all of White's pieces offside and d5 fully supported, Black finally decides that it is time to show his teeth. In fact, 21...d5 is the winning move.

22 exd5 e4 23 ♖e3 ♘xb3 24 cxb3 ♕c5 25 ♗c4 ♘xd5 26 ♘xd5 ♗xd5 27 ♗xd5 ♖xd5 28 f6 ♖d1+ 29 ♔f2 ♕f5+ 30 ♔g3 ♕e5+ 31 ♕f4 ♕xf4+ 32 ♔xf4 ♖f1+ 33 ♔g4 ♖xf6 34 ♖c3 ♖g6+ 35 ♔f4 ♖xg2 36 ♖c6 ♖g6 37 ♖xg6 fxg6 38 ♔e3 g5 39 ♖g3 ♔f7 40 ♖g2 ♔f6 41 ♖f2+ ♔e5 42 ♖f7 g6 43 b4 ♖e6 44 ♖a7 b5 45 axb5 axb5 46 ♖b7 ♖d6 47 ♖xb5+ ♖d5 48 ♖a5 g4 49 ♖a6 ♖d3+ 50 ♔e2 ♔f4 51 ♖a3 h5 52 b5 ♖xa3 53 bxa3 ♔e5 54 ♔e3 h4 55 b6 ♔d6 56 ♔xe4 g5 57 a4 h3!! 0-1 *(D)*

The final position deserves a diagram as it is one of the rare cases when one side has two connected passed pawns in a king and pawn endgame and is still completely lost!

7...②c6

This is an older but more solid option to the 7...♗c5 lines. White has two main choices which are covered in the annotated games – 8 ②xc6 and 8 ♗e3, both of which are good for a slight advantage. Having played both 7...♗c5 and 7...②c6, I personally prefer 7...♗c5 as it is relatively untested and White needs to be accurate. Nevertheless, 7...②c6 is a very solid option to which I revert when I am playing a particularly dangerous opponent.

Game 20
Tischbierek-Kamsky
New York 1991

1 e4 c5 2 ②f3 e6 3 d4 cxd4 4 ②xd4 a6 5 ②c3 ♕c7 6 ♗d3 ②f6 7 0-0 *(D)*

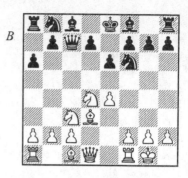

7 ...   ②c6

This time, Black challenges the knight on d4 with the knight on b8 with the difference that it gives White the option of exchanging the knight.

8 ②xc6

8 ♗e3 is the other major alternative and is discussed in the next annotated game. One of the problems I find with this line is that 8 ②xc6 is good for a small advantage to White and a line in which Black will find it hard to find winning attempts.

8 ②b3?! has been played but is obviously not in the spirit of things and Black has probably equalised already:

a) White lost very quickly in Mohd Kamal Abdullah-Juswanto, Jakarta Z 1993 after **8...♗e7 9 f4 d6 10 ♕f3 0-0 11 a4 b6 12 ♗e3 ♗b7 13 g4 ♖fe8 14 g5 ②d7 15 ♕h3 ②b4 16 f5? exf5 17 exf5 ②xd3 18 g6 ♗h4 19 ♕xh4 ♕c6!! 0-1.**

b) White again got very little joy in Botterill-Tal, Bath Echt 1973 after **8...b5 9 ♗g5 ♗e7 10 ♕e2 ♗b7 11 ♖ae1 d6 12 a3 b4 13 axb4 ♘xb4 14 ♖a1 0-0 15 ♘a5 ♗c8 16 ♗c4 ♖b8 17 f4 d5 18 e5 ♗c5+** and Black was fine and won in 51 moves.

8 ...   dxc6

The most popular way of recapturing on c6 though **8...bxc6** has its supporters:

a) **9 f4 d5:**

a1) In Hennigan-M.Schlosser, Oakham 1990 Black played an interesting exchange sacrifice: **10 ♔h1 ♗e7 11 e5 ♘d7 12 ♕h5 ♘c5 13 ♗e2 0-0 14 ♗e3 ♘d7 15 ♗d3 g6 16 ♕h6 f5 17 g4 ♖f7 18 gxf5 ♖xf5!? 19 ♗xf5 exf5 20 ♖g1 ♘f8 21 h4 ♗e6 22 h5 ♔f7 23 hxg6+ hxg6 24 ♘e2 c5 25 c3 ♖b8 26 ♖ab1 d4 27 cxd4 ♕c6+** ∓.

a2) A more classical approach was seen in Adams-Lobron, Munich 1993: **10 e5 ♘d7 11 ♘a4 ♘b6 12 ♘xb6 ♕xb6+ 13 ♔h1 g6 14 b3 a5 15 ♕e1 h5 16 ♗e3 c5 17 ♗f2 ♗e7 18 ♗h4 ♕d8 19 ♗xe7 ♕xe7 20 a3 ♗b7 21 h3 h4 22 ♔h2 ♔f8 23 c4 ♔g7 24 cxd5 ♗xd5 25 ♗e4 ♖hd8 26 ♗xd5 ♖xd5 27 ♖d1 ♖d4** ∓.

a3) White can also play more ambitiously as in the game Rohde-Spraggett, San Francisco 1987: **10 ♕f3 ♗e7 11 b3 0-0 12 ♗b2 ♖d8 13 e5 ♘d7 14 ♕h3 g6 15 ♘d1!? c5 16 c4 ♘b6 17 ♘f2 dxc4 18 bxc4 ♗b7 19 ♘g4 h5 20 ♘h6+ ♔g7 21 f5!! ♕c6 22 fxg6 ♔xh6 23 ♖xf7 ♖xd3 24 ♖h7+** 1-0.

b) Equally popular to 9 f4 is **9 ♕e2** with the following examples:

b1) **9...e5 10 f4 ♗d6 11 f5 ♗e7 12 ♔h1 ♗b7 13 ♗d2 d5 14 ♖ae1 ♘d7 15 ♕f3 ♘b6 16 a4 d4 17 a5 ♘c8 18 ♘a4 c5 19 b3 ♗c6 20 ♕g3 c4 21 ♕xg7 ♖f8 22 ♗e2 ♗xa4 23 bxa4 ♖b8 24 ♖b1 ♖xb1 25 ♖xb1 d3 26 cxd3 c3 27 ♖c1 c2 28 d4! ♗a3 29 ♗xa6! ♘a7 30 ♗h6!** ± was Nielsen-de la Riva, Buenos Aires 1992.

b2) **9...d5 10 ♗g5 ♗b7 11 f4 ♗e7 12 e5 ♘d7 13 ♗xe7 ♔xe7 14 ♘a4 c5 15 c4 d4 16 ♗e4 ♗xe4 17 ♕xe4 g6 18 b3 a5 19 ♘b2 h5 20 ♘d3 ♖a6 21 ♖ab1 ♖b8 22 ♖f2 ♖ab6 23 ♖fb2 ♔f8 24 h3 ♔g7 25 ♔f2 h4 26 ♔g1 ♖h8 27 ♕e1 ♖a6 28 ♖f2 ♘b6** ½-½ Spassky-Petrosian, Palma de Mallorca 1969.

It should be noted that after 8...dxc6, the position is very similar to the following line in the main line Kan after the moves 1 e4 c5 2 ♘f3 e6 3 d4 cxd4 4 ♘xd4 a6 5 ♗d3 ♘f6 6 0-0 ♕c7 7 c4?! ♘c6! 8 ♘xc6 dxc6 *(D)*:

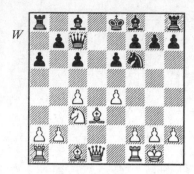

The only difference in the two lines is that in the above diagram, White has weakened d4 by playing c2-c4 whereas in this variation, the white pawn is on c2 and can thus still influence the d4-square.

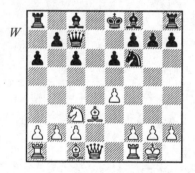

9 ♗g5

9 f4 e5 is the current main line:

a) **10 ♔h1:**

a1) Black played as if the white pawn were on c4 in Moulton-Motwani, Dublin Telecom 1991 with **10...♗c5** 11 f5 h5 12 ♕f3 b5! 13 ♗e3 ♕a7 14 ♖ae1 ♗b7 15 ♘d1 ♗xe3 16 ♘xe3 ♕d4 17

♕g3 ♖h7 18 ♘d1 0-0-0 19 ♖f3 c5 20 c3 ♕d6 21 b3 h4 22 ♕f2 c4 23 ♗c2 ♕d2 24 ♕xd2 ♖xd2 25 ♖f2 ♖d7 26 ♖fe2 cxb3 27 axb3 ♖h8 and Black had the advantage due to White's weak e4-pawn.

a1) **10..♗e7** did not work out well in Korneev-Vyzhmanavin, Moscow 1990: 11 a4 0-0 12 f5 h6 13 a5 ♗b4 14 ♕e1 ♖d8 15 g4 ♔f8?! 16 ♖g1 ♔e7? 17 ♗e3 c5 18 ♕h4 ±.

b) White got a slight positional disadvantage after **10 a4 ♘g4** 11 ♕e1?! exf4! 12 ♗xf4 ♘e5 13 ♕g3 f6 14 ♖ad1 ♗e6 15 ♔h1 0-0-0 16 ♗e2 ♗d6 in Watson-Bosbach, Bern 1990.

9 ...   ♗e7
10 a4   a5

The standard response to White's expansion on the queenside. Black cannot allow White to get a grip on b6 with a4-a5.

11 ♕e2   e5
12 ♗c4   h6
13 ♗e3?!

13 ♗d2! is better than the text as it cuts out Black's game plan.

13 ...   ♘g4
14 ♗d2 (D)   ♗g5!?

A sound positional move – Black exchanges his somewhat worse dark-squared bishop for White's counterpart. However, the move has the drawback that Black has not castled yet and is

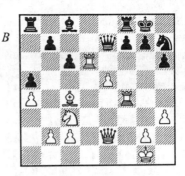

therefore susceptible to a direct attack on the king.

15	♖ad1	♕e7
16	h3	♘f6
17	f4	

The only way to continue playing for an advantage as if Black castles and develops his light squared bishop on c8 to e6, he has solved all his opening problems.

17	...	♗xf4
18	♗xf4	exf4
19	e5	♘h7

19...♘d7? 20 e6! fxe6 21 ♖xf4 and White has prevented Black from castling at the cost of a mere pawn.

| 20 | ♖xf4 | 0-0 |
| 21 | ♖d6 *(D)* | ♘g5!∓ |

The opening stages of the game are now over and White has made no impact on Black's solid structure. Instead, he is left with an isolated e-pawn which will be firmly blockaded by Black's knight.

22	♔h1	♘e6
23	♖f3	♕g5
24	♕e3	♕xe3
25	♖xe3	♖b8
26	♘e4?	

White should not allow this pawn break as his only compensation for his weak e-pawn is that Black's pieces are slightly congested on the queenside. Better was 26 ♔h2 followed by ♔g3, or 26 ♖ed3.

26	...	b5!
27	♗xe6	♗xe6
28	♘c5	♗f5
29	g4?	

Another bad decision, as Black will have full compensation for the exchange.

29	...	♗xc2
30	♘d7	bxa4
31	♘xb8	♖xb8
32	♖xc6	♖xb2
33	♔g1	♗b3!

Black protects his only weakness, f7, and at the same time

threatens to queen his passed a-pawn.

34 Ra6 a3 35 Rxa5 a2 36 Rc3 ♔h7 37 Ra6 ♗e6 38 Rca3 ♔g6 39 R6a5 ♔g5 40 R5a4 ♔h4 41 Ra5 Re2 42 ♔h1 g6 43 ♔g1 Rb2 44 R5a4 Re2 45 Ra5 a1♛+ 46 Rxa1 ♔xh3 47 ♔f1 Re4 48 g5 h5 49 R1a4 Rg4 50 Rxg4 ♔xg4 51 Ra3 ♔xg5 52 Rf3 ♔g4 53 Rf2 ♔g3! 0-1

A fine example of the kind of game to expect with 7...♘c6. Black is extremely solid and if White pushes too hard, Black can play for the win. However, I feel that White always has the option of retaining a very small edge throughout the game without taking any risks.

As Black, you must accept that White has the advantage, and in most defences, White has a 'boring' option which Black hates to face. It is safe to say that 8 ♘xc6 is dullest of White's continuations and the reader should be heartened by the fact that White mostly prefers 8 ♗e3 and the complications that arise from it to the less adventurous 8 ♘xc6. Black has two responses to 8 ♗e3: 8...♘e5 or 8...♗d6. The following games are a discussion of 8 ♗e3 and Black's possibilities.

Game 21
Mikhalchishin-Adler
Bled 1992

| 1 | e4 | c5 |
| 2 | ♘f3 | ♘c6 |

Although Black has played 2...♘c6, the game will transpose to the Kan.

3	d4	cxd4
4	♘xd4	♛c7
5	♘c3	e6
6	♗e3	a6
7	♗d3	♘f6
8	0-0 *(D)*	

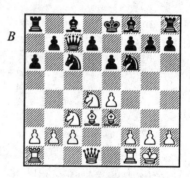

| 8 | ... | ♘e5 |

Kan players are more likely to reach the above position via the following move order: 1 e4 c5 2 ♘f3 e6 3 d4 cxd4 4 ♘xd4 a6 5 ♗d3 ♘f6 6 0-0 ♛c7 7 ♘c3 ♘c6 8 ♗e3.

The knight is immediately centralised where it attacks the bishop on d3 and has ideas of ...♘eg4 and ...♛xh2#.

8...♗d6 will be discussed in the next game.

9 h3

The best move to stop Black's threat of ...♘g4. White tried to retain his bishop pair but came off worse in Berzinš – Sideif-Zade, Naberczhnye Chelny 1993 after **9 ♗e2?! b5 10 f4 ♘c4! 11 ♗xc4 ♕xc4 12 e5 ♘d5 13 ♘xd5 ♕xd5 14 ♕e2 ♗b7 15 ♘b3 ♖c8** – Black's got the two bishops for nothing.

Two games have seen the retreat **9 ♘f3?!** though I can't see why this is should be good for an advantage:

a) **9...♘fg4 10 ♗f4 ♗d6 11 ♘d4 ♘xd3 12 ♗xd6 ♕xd6 13 ♘f3 b5 14 cxd3 ♗b7 15 h3 ♘e5 16 ♘xe5 ♕xe5 17 d4 ♕f4 18 a3 ♖c8 19 ♕d3 0-0 20 ♖ad1 f5 21 e5 ♖c7 22 ♖fe1 ♖fc8 23 ♖e3 ♕h4 24 ♖g3 h6 25 d5 ♖xc3! 26 bxc3 ♗xd5** and Black had all the winning chances in Timman-Ribli, Reykjavik 1988.

b) A riskier approach was adopted by Black in Jansa-Kveinys, Prague 1993: **9...♗d6!? 10 ♘xe5 ♗xe5 11 f4 ♗xc3 12 bxc3 ♕xc3 13 e5 ♘d5 14 ♗d2 ♕c5+ 15 ♔h1 b5 16 f5 ♗b7 17 fxe6 dxe6 18 ♕g4 h5 19 ♕xg7 0-0-0 20 ♕xf7 ♖hg8 21 ♖f2 ♘c7 22 ♖af1 h4** and Black had some compensation for the pawn. The Timman – Ribli example seems a better option for Black.

9 ...   ♗c5

Following the example of previous games when the bishop is posted outside of the pawn chain in order to enhance the ...e5 break. 9...♗c5 is criticised by Taimanov in *Winning With the Sicilian* as '...not in the spirit of the opening' and he goes on to give the one line example that after 10 ♘a4 ♗a7 11 c4 '...Black has a constrained game...' though 9...♗c5 has been employed by Grandmasters Anand, Timman and Ribli amongst others!

Taimanov prefers **9...b5!?** which is certainly more in the spirit of his philosophy on the Sicilian. Practical examples include:

a) Short-Illescas, Linares 1990 saw **10 f4 ♘c4 11 ♗xc4 ♕xc4 12 ♕d3** and then **12...♗b7?!** 13 a4 ♕xd3 14 cxd3 b4 15 ♘ce2 ♗c5 16 ♖fc1 and though Black has the two bishops, White's compact pawn structure and the use of the c-file give him a clear advantage. Taimanov mentions this possibility in his book and instead of 12...♗b7?! recommends **12...d5!** and gives the game Fischer-Petrosian, Santa Monica 1966 which continued 13 e5 ♘d7 14 ♕xc4 dxc4 15 f5!? ♘xe5 16 fxe6

♗xe6 17 ♖ae1 ♘d7!? 18 ♘xe6 fxe6 19 ♗d4 0-0-0 20 ♖xe6 ♘c5! 21 ♖c6+ ♔b7 22 ♖xc5 ♖xd4 23 ♖cf5 ♗d6 24 ♖f7+ ♔c6 25 ♖xg7 b4 when Black had compensation for the pawn.

b) After **10 ♕e2 b4 11 ♘b1 d5**:

b1) Schäfer-Schlosser, Münster 1992 saw **12 ♘d2 ♗b7 13 ♗g5 ♗e7 14 ♖fe1 0-0** and Black was fine. Another equalising line was seen in Dückstein-Taimanov, Copenhagen 1965 which went 12...dxe4 13 ♘xe4 ♘d5 =.

b2) **11 ♘d1 d5 12 ♗f4 ♗d6 13 ♗xe5 ♗xe5 14 ♘f3 ♗f4 15 exd5 ♘xd5 16 ♘e3 ♘xe3 17 fxe3 ♗h6 18 e4 0-0 19 e5 ♗b7** was Krogius-Taimanov, USSR Ch 1959 when Black had the advantage.

Returning to the position after 9...♗c5 *(D)*:

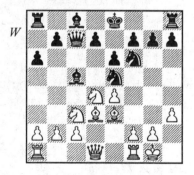

10   ♕e2

The other main option for White is to play **10 ♔h1 d6 11 f4**:

a) **11...♘c6?** 12 e5! ♘xe5 13 fxe5 dxe5 14 ♗b5+ axb5 15 ♘dxb5 ♕c6 16 ♗xc5 ♕xc5 17 ♘d6+ ♔e7 18 ♖xf6 gxf6 19 ♘ce4 ♕d4 20 ♕h5 ♖f8 21 ♖d1 ♕e3 22 ♕h4 ♕f4 23 ♕e1 ♖a4 24 ♕c3 ♖d4 25 ♖xd4 ♕f1+ 26 ♔h2 exd4 27 ♕c5 ♔d7 28 ♘b5 ♕f4+ 29 g3 1-0 was Kasparov-Anand, Tilburg 1991.

b) **11...♘ed7**:

b1) **12 a4 b6 13 ♕e1 ♗b7 14 ♕g3 g6 15 ♖ae1 ♘h5 16 ♕f2 0-0 17 ♘b3 ♗xe3 18 ♖xe3 e5 19 fxe5 dxe5 20 ♘d2 ♘c5 21 ♗c4 ♘f4** was Short-Ribli, Brussels SWIFT 1992 when Black was fully equal.

b2) **12 ♕f3 b5 13 ♕g3 ♗b7 14 a3**:

b21) Black fared well in Smagin-Matulović, Yugoslavia 1992 after **14...0-0** 15 ♕h4 ♕b6 16 ♕f2 e5 17 ♘f5 g6 18 fxe5 dxe5 19 ♗xc5 ♕xc5 20 ♘h6+ ♔g7 21 ♕d2 ♘h5 22 ♘f5+ ♔h8 23 ♗e2 ♘df6 24 ♕g5 ♘xe4 25 ♘xe4 ♗xe4 26 ♗xh5 f6 27 ♕h6 ♗xf5 28 ♖ad1 ♕e7 29 ♖d2 ♖ad8 30 ♖df2 ♕g7 31 ♕e3 ♗c8 32 ♗e2 f5 ∓.

d) Black played a little too freely with **14...h5?!** in Lau-Schlosser, Graz Z 1993 and got severely punished after 15 ♕f2 ♖c8 16 ♘f3 ♕b8 17 ♕h4 ♗xe3 18 ♖xe3 ♖c5 19 e5 ♘d5 20 ♘xd5

♗xd5 21 b4 ♖c3 22 cxd6 ♕xd6 23 f5 e5 24 ♘xe5 ♘xc5 25 ♖xe5+ ♕xe5 26 ♖e1 1-0.

10 ... d6 *(D)*

11 a4!?

More common is **11 f4 ♗g6**:

a) **12 ♕f2?!** 0-0 13 ♔h1 ♗d7 14 ♖ae1 ♖ac8 15 ♘b3 ♗xe3 16 ♕xe3 h6 17 e5 dxe5 18 fxe5 ♘h7 19 a4 ♖cd8 20 ♖f2 ♗c6 21 ♔g1 ♖fe8 22 ♘d2 ♘hf8 23 ♘c4 ♖e7 24 a5 when the weakness on b6 is compensated for by White's isolated e-pawn – Short-Ribli, Belfort 1988.

b) **12 ♘b3 ♗xe3+ 13 ♕xe3 b5**:

b1) **14 a3** 0-0 15 ♖ad1 ♗b7 16 ♖f2 ♖ad8 17 ♖fd2 e5 18 f5 ♘f4 19 ♗f1 d5 20 ♕c5! was ± in Timman-Illescas, Linares 1988.

b2) Timman showed the merits of Black's position in Kavalek-Timman, Prague 1990 after **14 ♖ae1** 0-0 15 g4?! ♕a7 16 e5 dxe5 17 fxe5 ♘d7 18 ♗xg6 hxg6 19 ♖f4 ♘b6 20 a4 ♕b8 21 ♘a5 ♗d7

22 ♖d4 ♕c7 23 axb5 axb5 24 b4 ♖fc8 25 ♖d3 ♗c8 26 ♖f1 ♖ab8 27 ♕g3 ♕e7 28 ♖d6 ♘c4 with an advantage to Black.

11 ... ♕b6!?

Or **11...0-0 12 a5** and then:

a) **12...♗d7** 13 f4 ♘xd3 14 cxd3 b5 15 axb6 ♕xb6 16 ♕f2 with a small advantage to White.

b) **12...♗b4** 13 ♘b3 ♗xc3 14 bxc3 ♕xc3 15 ♗d4 with compensation for the pawn.

12 a5 ♕a7

12...♕xb2? loses to 13 ♘a4 ♕b4 14 ♖fb1 ♕xa5 15 ♘xc5 ♕xc5 16 ♘xe6 with a winning advantage.

13 ♖ad1 *(D)*

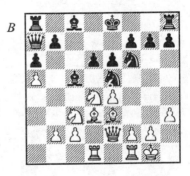

13 ... ♗d7!

Not **13...♗xd4??**, which loses to 14 ♗xd4 ♕xd4 15 ♗b5+!. Mikhalchishin also gives **13...0-0** 14 ♗c4 (intending b4!) 14...b5 15 axb6 ♕xb6 16 ♘a4±.

14 ♗c4

White tries to carry out the same idea as the previous note.

14 ... b5

14...♘xc4 15 ♕xc4 0-0 16 b4±.

15	axb6	♕xb6
16	♗b3	0-0
17	f4	♘c6
18	♕f2	♘xd4
19	♗xd4	♗c6
20	♗xc5?!	

Better was 20 ♖e1!, which would have denied the d5-square from Black. The game continuation still gives White a clear edge though Black's use of the d5-square gives him good chances of defending.

| 20 | ... | dxc5 |
| 21 | e5 | |

21 ♖e1 was again better.

21	...	♘e4
22	♘xe4	♗xe4
23	♖d6	♕b7
24	♕e2?	(D)

An inexplicable mistake as the obvious 24 ♖fd1 was far better.

| 24 | ... | a5! |

Though he has a clear positional disadvantage, Black continues to create as much trouble as possible.

| 25 | ♗a4 | c4! |

25...♖ab8 26 c4! intending ♗b5± – Mikhalchishin.

| 26 | ♖fd1 | ♗d5 |
| 27 | c3 | ♖fd8? |

27...♖ad8.

28 ♖xd8+?

28 ♗c6! ♕b6+ 29 ♕f2 ♕xf2+ 30 ♔xf2 ♖xd6 31 ♗xa8 ♖b6 32 ♖d2! ♔f8 33 ♗xd5 exd5 34 ♔e3±. Now Black has escaped the worst.

28	...	♖xd8
29	♖d2	g6
30	♕e3	♕e7
31	♕b6	♕h4
32	♕f2	♕e7!

32...♕xf2+ would have resulted in a pleasant endgame for White with 33 ♔xf2 intending ♔e3 and g4±.

| 33 | ♖d4 | ♖b8 |
| 34 | ♗d1? | |

34 ♔h2 intending g4 was still good for a slight edge.

34	...	a4!
35	♗xa4	♕a7
36	♕c2	♖a8
37	b3	cxb3
38	♗xb3	♖c8!=

39 ♔h2 ♕b6 40 ♖b4 ♕c5 41 ♕d2 ♕xc3 42 ♕xc3 ♖xc3 43 ♖b8+ ♔g7 44 ♗xd5 exd5 45 ♖d8 ♖d3 46 h4 h5 ½-½

Analysis based on notes by Mikhalchishin in *Informator 55*.

Game 22
Kasparov-Portisch
Debrecen Echt 1992

1 e4 c5 2 ♘f3 e6 3 d4 cxd4 4 ♘xd4 a6 5 ♘c3 ♛c7 6 ♗d3 ♘c6 7 ♗e3 ♘f6 8 0-0 *(D)*

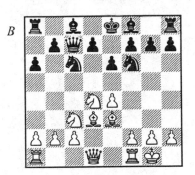

8 ...   ♗d6!? *(D)*

An interesting alternative to 8...♘e5 and one that has become popular amongst strong grandmasters. Black will not be able to stop White from playing f2-f4, but with 8...♗d6!? can at least buy some time for development.

9 ♘xc6

And here there is a major difference of opinion over White's best formation.

a) Equally popular to the text move is **9 h3** though Black seems to hold his own:

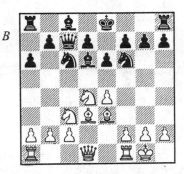

a1) Possibly the most unadventurous way to play for White was seen in Anand-Portisch, Brussels SWIFT 1992 after **9...♗h2+** 10 ♔h1 ♗f4 11 ♕c1 ♗xe3 12 ♕xe3 ♕b6 13 ♘f5 ♕xe3 14 ♘xe3 b5 15 a4 b4 16 ♘e2 ♖b8 17 f4 d6 18 a5 ♔e7 19 ♖fd1 ♖d8 20 ♘g3 ♗b7 21 ♖e1 ♔f8 22 ♔g1 g6 23 ♖a4 ♘d7 24 ♖aa1 ♘c5 and though Black went on to lose, he is no worse here.

a2) Black was again comfortable in Topalov-Lautier, Madrid 1993 after **9...♗f4** 10 ♗xf4 ♕xf4 11 ♘xc6 dxc6 12 a4 ♕o7 13 a5 c5 14 ♕d2 ♗e6 15 ♘a4 ♖d8 16 ♕c3 0-0 17 ♘c5 ♗c8 18 ♖ad1 ♘h5 19 ♗c4 ♘f4 20 b4 ♕e7 21 ♕f3 h5 22 c3 g5 23 ♘d3 ♘xd3 24 ♗xd3 h4 25 ♗c4 ♔g7 26 ♖xd8 ½-½

b) An interesting alternative is **9 ♔h1!?**:

b1) Marciano-Hjartarson, Reykjavik France-Iceland 1993 is one example: **9...h5** 10 ♘xc6

dxc6 11 f4 ♘g4 12 ♕e2 e5 13 f5
♕e7 14 ♘a4 b5 15 ♘b6 ♖b8 16
♘xc8 ♖xc8 17 a4 ♗c5 18 ♗xc5
♕xc5 19 g3 ♔e7 20 h3 ♘f6 21
♕f2?! ♕xf2 22 ♖xf2 ♖hd8 =
though I feel that had White kept
the queens on the board, he would
have had some advantage.

b2) A more classical approach
by Black was seen in Shmuter-
Brodsky, Ukrainian Ch (Sim-
feropol) 1990 which was a
transposition again (1 e4 c5 2
♘f3 ♘c6 3 d4 cxd4 4 ♘xd4 ♕c7
5 ♘c3 e6 6 ♗e3 a6 7 ♗d3 ♘f6 8
0-0 ♗d6): 9...♗e5 10 ♘b3 ♗f4
11 ♕d2 ♗xe3 12 ♕xe3 b5 13 f4
d6 14 a4 b4 15 ♘e2 0-0 16 a5
e5?! (better was 16...♗b7 with
...e5 in mind; now the a-pawn is
weak) 17 fxe5 ♘g4 18 ♕g3
♘gxe5 19 ♘f4 ♗e6 20 ♘xe6
fxe6 21 ♖xf8+ ♖xf8 22 ♗xa6±.

9 ...   bxc6

9...dxc6 10 f4 e5 11 f5 is also
played:

a) **11...b5** 12 a4 ♖b8 13 ♔h1
0-0 14 ♖f3 ♖d8 15 ♖h3 h6 16
axb5 axb5 17 ♕e1 ♗e7 18 ♕g3
♔f8 19 ♗xh6! gxh6 20 ♖xh6
♔e8 21 ♕g7 ♕d6 22 ♖h8+ ♔d7
23 ♖xd8+ ♗xd8 24 ♗xb5 cxb5
25 ♖d1 ± Ivanchuk-J.Polgar,
Melody Amber blindfold 1993.

b) **11...♕e7 12 ♔h1** and now:

b1) **12...b5** 13 a4 ♗b7 14 ♕f3
♗c5 15 ♗g5 h6 16 ♗h4 ♖d8 17

♘e2 ♕c7 18 ♕g3 with an advantage to White in Garcia-Zapata,
Cali Z 1990.

b2) Zapata improved in the
game Sieiro Gonzalez-Zapata,
Havana 1990 with **12...h6!?** 13
♘a4 b5 14 ♘b6 ♖b8 15 ♘xc8
♖xc8 16 ♕f3 ♗c5 17 ♗d2 ♖d8
18 a4 0-0 19 ♕g3 ♖d6 20 axb5
cxb5 21 ♕h4 ♖e8 22 ♖f3 ♘h7 23
♕g4 ♘f6 24 ♕h4 ½-½.

10 f4   e5
11 f5 (D)

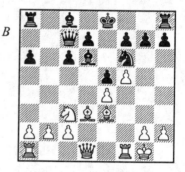

11 ...   ♗e7

Gheorghiu preferred **11...♗b4**
12 ♘a4 d5 13 ♕f3 ♖b8 14 c4 d4
15 ♗g5 ♘d7 16 a3 ♗d6 17 f6 g6
18 c5 ♘xc5 19 ♘xc5 ♗xc5 20 b4
♗d6 21 ♖fc1 a5 22 b5 c5 23 ♗c4
a4 24 ♖ab1 ♗e6 25 ♗xe6 fxe6
26 ♕d3 in Sznapik-Gheorghiu,
Thessaloniki OL 1988 when
White had compensation for the
sacrificed pawn.

12 ♘a4!?   d5
13 ♗b6   ♕b8

14	♕e2	c5!?
15	♗xc5?!	

Portisch points out **15 c4!** ♘d7 (15...♗d7 16 ♗c2 dxc4 17 ♗a5 allows White a small advantage) 16 ♗a5 d4 =. Instead, Kasparov sacrifices the exchange for very little in return.

15	...	♗xc5+
16	♘xc5	♕b6 *(D)*

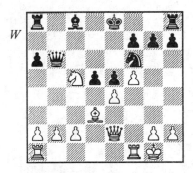

17	♕f2	

17 ♕e3? ♘g4 18 ♕g5 ♕xc5+ 19 ♔h1 h5 20 h3 ♗b7∓.

17	...	♘g4
18	♘a4	♕xf2+
19	♖xf2	♘xf2
20	♔xf2	d4
21	b4	♗d7
22	♘c5!	♗b5
23	a4!	♗xd3
24	cxd3	♔e7
25	♖c1!	

Realising that his exchange sacrifice has not paid off, Kasparov poses as many technical problems for Black as possible. Although the endgame is clearly better for Black, the lack of open files means that Black's rooks are not effective.

25	...	♖hc8
26	♖c4	♖c6
27	a5	

Closing one front. Black can now only hope for a break on the kingside.

27	...	♖b8
28	♔e2	♔d6
29	h4? *(D)*	

A careless move which nearly lets White's barrier slip. **29 g4!** would have made Black's task much harder, if at all possible.

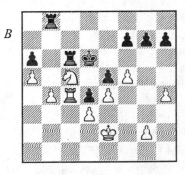

29	...	h5!
30	♔f3	♖b5?

Black misses his chance to break with **30...g6!** when after 31 g4 gxf5 32 gxf5 ♖g8 33 ♖c1 ♖g4 34 ♖h1 White would be grimly holding.

31	g4	g6
32	g5!	♖b8

33	f6	♖b5
34	♔e2	♖cxc5
35	bxc5+	♔c6
36	♖a4	♖xc5
37	♖a2	♖b5

½-½

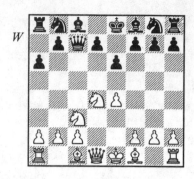

White plays ♗e2

Occasionally, White develops his light-squared bishop on e2 instead of the more aggressive d3. This plan is usually adopted when White has only learnt one system against the Kan, the Taimanov, Najdorf and the Scheveningen Sicilians and always places his bishop on e2. It is now well-known that one of the 'drawbacks' of the Kan is that the light-squared bishop is allowed to go to d3 whereas in other Sicilians, Black does not allow this possibility. Thus the ♗e2 lines are rare in the Kan in that everyone who plays White in the Sicilian knows up to 5 ♗d3!

If White wants to play his bishop to e2, he must make his choice on move 6 after 1 e4 c5 2 ♘f3 e5 3 d4 cxd4 4 ♘xd4 a6 5 ♘c3 ♛c7 *(D)*. Now White has to reveal his formation by playing 6 ♗e2. But what of Black's responses? Unfortunately, Black has a host of possibilities and a thorough evaluation of each of

these possibilities would take up a chapter on its own! However, the current consensus is that one particular line, 8...♗b4!, is fine for Black.

Game 23
Kamsky-Ehlvest
Linares 1991

1 e4 c5 2 ♘f3 e6 3 d4 cxd4 4 ♘xd4 ♘c6 5 ♘c3 ♛c7 6 ♗e3 a6 7 ♗e2 ♘f6 8 0-0 *(D)*

8 ... ♗b4!

Kan players would reach this position via the move-order 1 e4 c5 2 ♘f3 e6 3 d4 cxd4 4 ♘xd4 a6 5 ♘c3 ♕c7 6 ♗e2 ♘f6 7 0-0 ♘c6 8 ♗e3 ♗b4!.

9 ♘a4

The main line and the only way for White to play for an advantage. Other recent alternatives include: **9 ♘xc6 bxc6 10 ♘a4 0-0 11 f4** (11 ♘b6 transposes to the game) and now:

a) **11...♗e7** 12 ♗f3 ♖b8 13 c4 d6 14 ♕d2 c5 15 ♖ad1 ♗b7 16 ♘c3 ♖bd8 17 ♕f2 ♘d7 18 ♖d3 ♘b8 19 ♖fd1 ♘c6 20 b3 ♖fe8 21 ♔h1 ♗f6 22 ♘c2 g6 23 ♖3d2 ♗g7 24 ♕h4 ♘e7 25 ♕f2 ♘c6 26 ♕h4 ♗f8 27 ♘c3 ♘e7 28 ♕f2 ♗g7 29 ♘e2 ♘c6 ½-½ was Khalifman-Salov, Wijk aan Zee Ct 1994. A comfortable draw for Black and a game which highlighted the merits of the Kan/Taimanov systems.

b) A worse way for Black to play the position is **11...♖b8** 12 ♗d3 d5 as in Dolmatov-Polgar, Polanica Zdroj 1991, which went 13 e5 ♘d7 14 c4 ♗e7 15 ♕c2 h6 16 cxd5 exd5 17 ♖ac1 ♗b7 18 ♗f5 a5 19 e6 fxe6 20 ♗xe6+ ♔h8 21 ♗xd5 ±.

9 ...   0-0

a) **9...♗e7** is an Ulf Andersson speciality but one that I highly recommend Black avoid unless you possess Andersson's defensive qualities. **10 ♘xc6 bxc6 11** ♘b6 ♖b8 12 ♘xc8 ♕xc8 13 e5 ♘d5 14 ♗c1 ♗c5 15 c4 ♘e7 and now:

a1) **16 ♔h1** 0-0 17 b3 ♕c7 18 ♗b2 ♘g6 19 ♗d3 ♖bd8 20 ♕h5 d6 21 exd6 ♗xd6 22 ♖ad1 c5 23 g3 ♖fe8 24 f4 ♕c6+ 25 ♔g1 f5 26 ♗e2 ♗e7 and though the position is equal, White has all the winning chances; Bouaziz-Andersson, Szirak IZ 1987.

a2) **16 b3** ♕c7 17 ♗b2 ♘g6 18 ♕d3 0-0 19 ♕e4 f5 20 exf6 gxf6 21 ♖ad1 ♕f4 22 ♕c2 ♖f7 23 g3 was Dolmatov-Kotronias, Reykjavik 1988 and White again had a nagging edge.

b) Another older line is **9...b5?!** which has since been busted by the game Renet-Lautier, Lyon Z 1990 which went 10 ♘xc6 dxc6 11 ♗c5 bxa4 12 ♗xb4 c5 13 ♗a3! ♘xe4 14 ♗f3 ♗b7 15 ♖e1 ♘d6 16 ♖e5 ♖d8 17 ♖xc5±.

10 ♘xc6

The gambit line **10 c4!?** is the subject of the next annotated game.

10 ...   bxc6

For once **10...dxc6?** is not playable. White has enormous compensation for the pawn after 11 c4! ♗d6 12 f4 ♘xe4 13 c5 ♗e7 14 ♕c2 f5 15 ♘b6 ♖b8 16 ♗d3 ♘f6 17 ♗d4±.

11	♘b6	♖b8
12	♘xc8	♖fxc8

13   ♗xa6 (D)

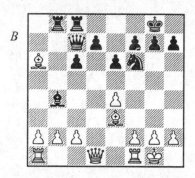

13   ...   ♖f8

There is some debate as to where to the rook should be placed. In *Winning with the Sicilian*, Taimanov played **13...♖e8?!** but then commented that theory now says that the rook should be on d8. The very latest theory, however, considers the best square for the rook to be f8, where it can sometimes help defend the king.

14   ♗d3   ♗d6
15   g3!?

15 f4 is the most popular move, but it is interesting that Kamsky gives this move a ?! in his *Informator 51* notes. 15 f4 is usually followed up by a kingside pawn storm with g4 and Kamsky obviously believes in Black's defences. Practical examples also seem to point in Black's favour after **15...e5**:

a) **16 f5 ♖xb2 17 g4 ♕a5 18 ♔h1 ♗c5** and now:

a1) **19 ♗c1 ♖xa2 20 ♖xa2 ♕xa2 21 g5 ♘e8 22 ♕e2 ♘d6 23 ♕g4 g6 24 fxg6 fxg6 25 ♕xd7 ♖xf1+ 26 ♗xf1 ♕xc2 27 ♕d8+ ♔f7 28 ♕f6+ ♔g8 29 ♕d8+ ♔f7 30 ♕f6+ ♔g8 31 ♕d8+ ♔f7 32 ♕f6+ ♔e8 33 ♕xe5+ ♔d8 34 ♕f6+ ♔c8 35 ♕f8+ ♔b7 36 ♕e7+ ♔b6 37 ♕d8+ ♔b7 38 ♕d7+ ♔b6 ½-½** Hartmann-Bischoff, Bundesliga 1986.

a2) **19 ♗xc5 ♕xc5 20 g5 ♘e8 21 ♕c1 ♖b4 22 a3 ♖d4 23 g6 d5 24 gxh7+ ♔xh7 25 f6 dxe4 26 fxg7 ♘xg7 27 ♖g1 f6 28 ♗e2 ♖d7 29 ♕f1 f5** and the players agreed a draw though Black is better.

b) Illescas-P.Cramling, Tarrasa 1990 saw a different approach by White but the same result: **16 b3 exf4 17 ♗d4 f3 18 e5 f2+ 19 ♖xf2 ♗xe5 20 ♗xe5 ♕xe5 21 ♔h1 ♖be8 22 ♖f5 ♕c3 23 ♖f3 ♕e5 24 ♖f5 ♕c3 25 ♖f3 ♕e5 ½-½**.

15   ...   ♗e5 (D)
15...♖xb2!? 16 ♗d4 ♖b4! 17 c3 ♖b2+ 17 ♗xf6 gxf6 18 ♕g4+ ♔h8 19 ♕h4 ♗e5?! 20 ♖ad1 c5?! 21 f4 ♗d4+?! 22 ♔h1 c4 23 ♗e2 ♗c3 24 ♖f3 ♗b2 25 g4± – Kamsky.

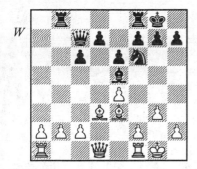

16 a4!?

The exchange sacrifice is insufficient after **16 b3?!** ♗xa1 17 ♕xa1 d5 18 e5 ♘d7 19 f4 c5 20 c4 d4 21 ♗d2 f6 22 exf6 ♖xf6 intending ...e5∓.

16 ...   ♗xb2
17 ♖a2+

17 ♖b1 would be met by 17...d5 18 exd5 cxd5 19 ♗b5 ♗c3 and Black has the advantage.

17 ...   d5
18 exd5   ♘xd5?!

A strange decision which leaves Black with a weak c-pawn. Clearly better and more natural was **18...cxd5** 19 a5 d4 20 ♗d2 e5.

19 ♗d2   ♖fd8
20 a5?!

Better was **20 c4** ♘f6 with a small advantage to White. 20...♘c3 would be met by 21 ♗xc3 ♗xc3 22 ♗xh7+!.

20 ...   ♗c3

Kamsky points out **20...♘c3!** 21 ♗xc3 ♗xc3 22 a6 ♗d4 23 ♕f3 when White's a-pawn gives him the edge but the opposite-coloured bishops enable Black to hold.

21 ♖a4!?   ♖b4
22 ♖a3!?   ♗xd2
23 ♕xd2   ♖db8
24 a6   ♕a7
25 ♕e2   h6
26 ♕e5   ♖4b6?!
27 c4!   ♘f6

27...♘b4? 28 c5 ♘xd3 29 cxb6 is winning for White.

28 c5 ♖b2 29 ♕d6 ♘d5 30 ♖c1 ♖c8 31 ♖a4 ♖bb8 32 ♕e5 ♘f6 33 ♖f4?! ♖d8 34 ♖d4 ♖xd4 35 ♕xd4 ♘d5 36 ♕e4 g6 37 ♕e5 ♘b4?! 38 ♗f1 ♖d8 39 ♕f4 ♘d3 40 ♕d2 ♕a6 41 ♖d1 ♘d5 40 ♕xh6± ♖b8 41 h4 ♖b2 42 h5 ♘f6? 43 ♖d1! ♕e7 44 hxg6 ♖xf2

44...fxg6 45 ♕xg6+ ♔f8 46 ♖b1! ±

45 g7 ♖h2 46 ♕xh2 1-0

A win for White but Black had numerous chances and was certainly no worse out of the opening. Clearly, Black has nothing to fear in these lines but there is one dangerous gambit line in this system that, from personal experience, I recommend everyone should beware of.

Game 24
Busquets-Mortazavi
San Francisco 1994

1 e4 c5 2 ♘f3 e6 3 d4 cxd4 4 ♘xd4 ♘c6 5 ♘c3 ♕c7 6 ♗e2 ♘f6 7 0-0 a6 8 ♗e3 ♗b4 9 ♘a4 0-0 *(D)*

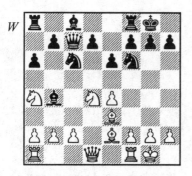

10 c4!?

A dangerous pawn sacrifice which no one had mentioned to me in my pre-game analysis! Taimanov merely mentions the move as '...deserving of consideration...' but stops there and thus I had never really paid much attention to its dangers. I casually played...

10 ... ♗d6?!

A very risky move. The bishop merely hinders Black's development at the cost of a pawn which White is happy to give away for the fearsome attack that he generates.

10...♗e7! is a far better option and Black is only a little worse:

a) Känel-Nemet, Swiss Ch 1988 saw 11 ♘xc6 bxc6 12 ♕c2 c5 13 f4 d6 14 ♖ae1 ♗b7 15 ♗d3 h6 16 ♘c3 ♖ad8 17 ♗c1 ♘d7 and we have a similar position to the Khalifman-Salov game (see previous annotated game) where Black comfortably held his own with the manoeuvre ...♖fe8, ...g6 and ...♗g7.

b) In Todorović-Ninov, Novi Sad 1992, White played 11 ♘c3!? d6 12 ♖c1 ♘e5 13 f4 ♘g6 14 f5 ♘e5 15 g4 h6 16 g5 hxg5 17 ♗xg5 ♘h7 18 ♗e3 ♕d8 19 ♕d2 ♗g5 20 ♔h1 ♗d7 21 ♖g1 ♗xe3 22 ♕xe3 ♕h4 and Black averted mate and won in 66 moves.

11 f4!

The most direct route. **11 g3 ♘xe4 12 ♗f3** has also been played:

a) **12...♘f6** 13 c5 ♘xd4 14 ♗xd4 ♗e7 15 ♖c1 d5 16 cxd6 ♕xd6 17 ♘b6 e5 18 ♗c5 ♕xd1 19 ♖fxd1 ♗xc5 20 ♖xc5 ♖b8 21 ♘xc8 ♖fxc8 22 ♖xc8+ ♖xc8 23 ♗xb7 ♖b8 24 ♗xa6 ± Todorović-Sokolov, Yugoslav Ch 1988.

b) **12...f5** 13 c5! ♗e5 14 ♘b6 ♖b8 15 ♗xe4 fxe4 16 ♘c4 ♗f6 17 ♖c1! ± Gufeld-Conquest, Hastings 1986.

11	...	♘xe4
12	♘xc6	bxc6
13	♗d3	♘f6?!

13...f5 was the other option but White would still be on top after 14 ♕f3 ♘f6 15 c5 ♗e7 16 ♗d4 with the dual threats of ♘b6 and ♗e5.

14 c5

a) 14 ♗b6 ♕b8 15 ♗d5 e5?! (better is 15...♗e7 when White has compensation after 16 c5!) 16 ♗c3! c5?! 17 fxe5 ♗xe5 18 ♖xf6! ♗xf6 19 ♗xf6 ♕f4 20 ♗c3 ± Rogers-Van Mil, Wijk aan Zee 1992.

b) 14 ♘b6?! ♖b8 15 ♘xc8 ♖fxc8 16 c5 ♗e7 17 ♗xa6 ♖d8 18 ♕c1 ♘d5 19 ♗d4 ♕a7! 20 ♗d3 ♖d4 and Black was fine in Obukhov-Tregubov, Sochi 1993.

14	...	♗e7
15	♗d4 *(D)*	

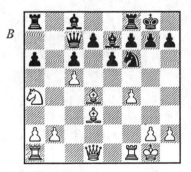

| 15 | ... | ♘d5?? |

15...♖d8! was the only move, when White has a huge initiative

but at least it is not forced checkmate.

16	♘b6	♘xb6
17	♗xh7+!!	♔xh7
18	♕h5+	♔g8
19	♗xg7 *(D)*	

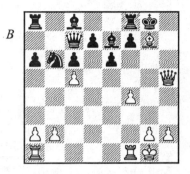

| 19 | ... | f5 |

A terrible sight. White has sacrificed three pieces in the most spectacular fashion. After the game, my opponent made me feel much better by informing me that the entire game had once been played somewhere in the USSR between Tal and Kuzmin! He was incorrect on both counts as I have since found two games which reached the diagrammed position and Kuzmin never played Tal, but Sveshnikov!

In Kuzmin-Sveshnikov, USSR 1973, Black played **19...♔xg7** 20 ♕g5+ ♔h7 21 ♖f3 ♗c5+ 22 ♔h1 1-0. Borocz-Fogarasi, Hungarian Ch 1991 instead went **19...f6** 20 ♕g6 ♗xc5+ 21 ♔h1 ♖f7 22

♗h6+ 1-0. Both these games lasted twenty-two moves but, personally, I could not be bothered with the formalities of ...♗xc5+ and ♔h1 and after ...

20 ♕g6

... I resigned.

1-0

I used to think that chess games were unique at this level but this game came mighty close.

Other 7th move options for White

Game 25
Gullaksen-Stefansson
Gausdal Arnold Cup 1993

1 e4 c5 2 ♘f3 e6 3 d4 cxd4 4 ♘xd4 a6 5 ♗d3 ♘f6 6 0-0 ♕c7 (D)

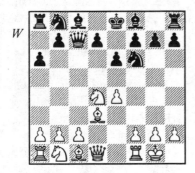

7 ♘d2!?

The philosophy behind this move is to retain the dangerous knight on d4 by supporting it via ♘d2, f4 and ♘df3. Other 7th move options include **7 ♔h1** – a dangerous move which can trick Black into a bad version of the Maroczy Bind. For example:

a) **7...♗e7?!** 8 f4 d6 9 c4! 0-0 10 ♘c3 ♘bd7 11 ♕e2 b6 12 ♗d2 ♗b7 was Vujačić-Plachetka, Belgrade 1984 and we have a similar position to the Nunn-Gheorghiu encounters (see main line chapter) which are very dangerous for Black. In the Plachetka game, White played the rather tame 13 ♖ac1?! instead of the more direct 13 ♖ae1! with the idea of an immediate e5.

b) As White has not yet committed his queen's knight to c3, **7...♗c5** will result in similar positions to the above option after 8 ♘b3 ♗e7 and White will play c4 and achieve the same favourable set-up.

c) **7...b5?!** has been played but does not seem to make any sense as White's knight is again not on c3. 8 f4 ♗b7 9 ♕e2 ♘c6 10 ♘xc6 ♕xc6 11 ♘d2 ♗e7 12 e5 ♘d5 13 c4! ♘b4 14 ♗e4 ♕b6 15 c5! ♗xc5 16 ♗xb7 ♕xb7 17 ♘e4 ♗e7 18 f5 0-0-0 19 ♗g5! d5 20 exd6 ♗xd6 21 ♗xd8 ♗b8 22 fxe6 fxe6 23 ♗a5 ♘c6 24 ♖ac1 ♗c7 25 ♗xc7 ♕xc7 26 ♖c3 ♔b8 27 ♖fc1 ♘d4 28 ♕f2 ♕e5 29 ♖d1 b4 30 ♖e3 ♕f5 31 ♕g3+

♔a8 32 ♕xg7 ♖f8 33 h3 e5 34 ♘c5 1-0 was a resounding victory for White in Chiburdanidze-Vyzhmanavin, Kusadasi 1990.

d) In my opinion, there are only two moves which can give Black a reasonable game. The first of these is **7...♘c6** and after 8 ♘xc6 bxc6 we reach previously seen positions as in Van der Wiel-Hulak, Wijk aan Zee 1987 which went 8 ♘xc6 bxc6 9 f4 d5 10 ♘d2 ♗e7 11 b3 0-0 12 ♗b2 a5 13 ♕f3 a4 with roughly equal chances for both sides.

e) Perhaps more in the spirit of the Kan is the more ambitious **7...g6!?**. There have been no practical examples of this move. The game M.Schlosser-Vyzhmanavin, Sochi 1989 went 7 ♕e2 d6 8 f4 g6 9 f5 ♗g7 10 fxe6 fxe6 11 ♗c4 ♘c6! and Black held his own. Here, instead of 7 ♕e2, White has played 7 ♔h1 and thus Black should be able to get away with 7...g6!?.

Other 7th move options are dubious and rarely seen. One popular line patented by Hungarian Grandmaster Gyula Sax, was 7 **f4?!** though in the game Sax-Bellon, Graz 1984 Black secured a good game after 7...♗c5 8 c3 ♘c6 9 e5 ♘d5 10 ♗e4 d6 11 ♗xd5 exd5 12 exd6 ♗xd6 13 ♖e1+ ♘e7 14 ♕f3 0-0 15 ♗e3 ♘f5 16 g3 ♖e8 17 ♘d2 ♘xe3 18 ♖xe3 ♖xe3 19 ♕xe3 ♗d7 20 ♕f3 ♖e8∓ and went on to win in 43 moves.

7 **♗e3** is a speciality of the computer software program MChessPro though I cannot see why the software authors did not stick to main line. The easiest road to equality is **7...d5!** 8 ♘c3 dxe4 9 ♘xe4 ♘bd7 10 ♘xf6+ ♘xf6 11 ♕f3 ♗d6 12 h3 0-0 13 ♖ad1 ♗d7 14 ♖fe1 ♖ae8 15 ♗g5 ♗e5 16 ♗f1 ♘d5 17 c3 b5 18 ♕e4 ♗h2+ 19 ♔h1 ♗f4 20 ♗xf4 ♘xf4 21 ♘f3 ♗c6 22 ♕e5 ♖e7 23 ♕xc7 ♖xc7 24 ♖e3 ♗d5 ½-½, as in Ernst-Lau, Dortmund 1992. Black can play more ambitiously by selecting any of the 'normal' developing moves such as **7...♗c5** or even **7...g6**.

7 **b3** was given a try by Nigel Short but I'm sure that he will not be trying it again after the game Short-Sax, Arnhem-Amsterdam 1983: 7...d6 8 ♗b2 ♘bd7 9 c4 g6 10 ♘c3 ♗g7 11 ♕e2 0-0 12 ♖ad1 b6 13 ♗b1 ♗b7 14 ♔h1 ♖fe8 15 f4 e5! 16 fxe5 ♘xe5 17 ♖de1 b5 18 cxb5 d5! 19 ♖xf6 ♗xf6 20 bxa6 ♗xa6 21 ♘xd5 ♕d6 22 ♘b5 ♗xb5 23 ♘xf6+ ♕xf6 24 ♕xb5 ♕f2 25 ♗c3 ♘g4 26 ♕g5

♖ac8 27 ♗b4 ♕d4 28 ♕xg4 ♕xb4∓.

7 ... g6!

The correct response. White will have to waste a move with the ♘b1-d2-f3 manoeuvre and thereby Black has the chance to also 'waste' a move and fianchetto his bishop.

In fact, 7...g6! is directed against White's set-up which will eventually involve some sort of kingside attack with f4 and ♕e1-h4. 7 ♘d2, however, gives Black time to blunt the influence of the d3-bishop, which in normal circumstances would be a potent attacking force against Black's vulnerable h7-pawn. Now, the bishop is biting at granite and Black has not conceded any development time as White has also wasted a move.

7...g6! is a recent novelty and there have been many other moves played by Black:

a) The most popular is the 'natural' **7...d6**, e.g. **8 f4** and now:

a1) Black ignored White's 7th move and played a standard Scheveningen type set-up in Szalanczy-Velikov, Graz 1987 after **8...♘bd7** 9 ♕e2 ♗e7 10 ♘2f3 ♘c5 11 ♗d2 0-0 12 e5 ♘e8 13 ♖ae1 b5 14 ♔h1 g6 15 ♕f2 ♘g7 16 ♕g3 ♘xd3 17 cxd3 ♗b7

18 ♘g5 ♕d7 19 ♘df3 ♖ac8 20 ♗c3 with a dangerous attack.

a2) In Füsthy-Hulak, Berlin 1988, Black again fianchettoed and had a good game after **8...g6** 9 ♘2f3 ♗g7 10 ♕e1 ♘bd7 11 ♗d2 0-0 12 ♕h4 e5 13 fxe5 dxe5 14 ♘b3 ♘h5 15 ♔h1 h6 16 ♗b4 ♖e8 17 ♘bd2 ♘c5 18 ♗c4 ♗e6 19 ♕e1 b5 20 ♕e3 ♗xc4 21 ♘xc4 ♘xe4 22 ♕xe4 ♕xc4 23 ♕xc4 bxc4 24 ♘d2 ♖ac8 25 ♘e4 ♖c6 and Black's central pawns decisively rolled forward.

b) The most solid option is to play *à la* Taimanov **7...♘c6**. A typical game in this line is Tukmakov-Karpov, USSR 1973 which went 8 ♘xc6 bxc6 9 f4 d5 10 b3 ♗e7 11 ♗b2 a5 12 c4 0-0 13 ♕c2 h6 and the position was roughly equal.

c) The immediate equalising attempt **7...d5?!** does not seem good enough. Although Black will not necessarily get mated, the lost time will eventually catch up with him in a strategic struggle. Rodriguez-Fernandez, Novi Sad OL 1990 saw 8 ♕e2 dxe4 9 ♘xe4 ♘bd7 10 c4 ♗e7 11 b3 ♘xe4 12 ♗xe4 ♘c5 13 ♗c2 ♗f6 14 ♗b2 0-0 15 ♖ad1 ♖b8 16 ♖fe1 g6 17 ♘b5 ♕e7 18 ♗e5 ♗xe5 19 ♕xe5 ♘d7 20 ♕d6 ♕xd6 21 ♘xd6 ♘f6 22 ♘e4 ♔g7 23 ♖d6 ♖e8 24 ♘xf6 ♔xf6 25 c5

♔e7 26 ♖ed1 ♖a8 27 ♗e4 ♖a7 28 f4 a5 29 ♔f2 h6 30 h4 ♖g8 31 g3 g5 32 ♔f3 gxh4 33 gxh4 1-0. Black really did not have a chance.

d) I like the look of **7...♗c5** but am slightly worried about 8 c3 though all practical examples have seen 8 ♘2b3?!, in which case we can retreat the bishop to e7 as in the main line.

Clearly, these options are playable but I see nothing wrong with 7...g6! which seems to stop White's idea in its tracks.

8 ♖e1?!

White does not really test Black's novelty. Although I think that Black has sound defences against the more traditional attacking formations, White should really have tried something like **8 ♔h1 ♗g7 9 f4 d6 10 ♘2f3 0-0 11 ♕e2 b6!** (there is no need for 11...b5?! as White does not have a knight on c3) **12 ♗d2 ♗b7 13 ♖ac1 ♘bd7 14 ♕f2 e5!** and Black is fine.

8	...	d6
9	♘2f3	♘bd7
10	a4	♗g7

10...b6 was tempting but perhaps Black was slightly worried about his development. White may also have the annoying 11 a5! b5 (11...bxa5 12 ♗d2 is good for White) when Black will find

it hard to play 12...♗g7 as White has ideas of 13 ♗xb5 axb5 14 ♘xb5 and ♘xd6+ with full compensation for the piece.

11	a5	0-0
12	♗g5	h6
13	♗d2	♘c5
14	♖a3	♖d8
15	b4	♘xd3
16	cxd3 *(D)*	

16	...	e5!

A theme with which the reader will be familiar with now. Black is perfectly placed for this break as the ...d5-thrust is well prepared and White does not have any way to overprotect this square.

17	♖c3	♕e7
18	♘b3	♗d7
19	♕b1	♗c6!

Everything is now directed at d5.

20	♗e3	♖e8
21	♖cc1 *(D)*	

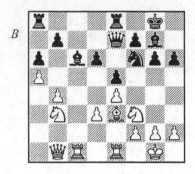

21	...	d5
22	♘c5	♖ac8
23	h3	♚h7
24	♖ed1	♖c7
25	♘h2	♖ec8
26	f3	♘h5!

A theme often seen in the King's Indian Defence. The black knight will go to f4 and ♗xf4 is answered with ...exf4 when Black's dark-squared bishop is unleashed on the a1-h8 diagonal.

27 ♕a2 ♕d6 28 ♕f2 d4 29 ♗d2 f5 30 g4 fxg4 31 hxg4 ♘f4 32 ♗xf4 exf4 33 ♘f1 ♗b5 34 ♕a2 ♕f6 35 ♘d2 h5! 36 gxh5 ♕g5+ 37 ♚h1 ♕xh5+ 38 ♚g2 ♕g5+ 39 ♚h2 ♕h4+ 40 ♚g2 ♕g3+ 41 ♚h1 ♕h3+ 42 ♚g1 ♕g3+ 43 ♚h1 ♗f8 44 ♘db3 ♕xf3+ ∓

44...♚h8 seems to force mate but White has the defence 45 ♕g2!.

45 ♕g2 ♕h5+ 46 ♕h2 ♕xh2+ 47 ♚xh2 g5 48 ♘xd4 ♗xc5 49

bxc5 ♖xc5 50 ♖xc5 ♖xc5 51 ♘xb5 axb5 52 d4 ♖c2+ 53 ♚h3 ♚g6 54 ♖b1 ♖c3+ 55 ♚g2 g4 56 ♖xb5 ♖c2+ 57 ♚f1 f3 58 ♖f5 ♖e2 59 d5 ♖xe4 60 ♖f8 ♚g5 61 d6 ♖d4 62 ♚f2 ♖d2+ 0-1

White castles queenside

Game 26
Tolnai-J.Polgar
Hungarian Ch 1991

1 e4 c5 2 ♘f3 e6 3 d4 cxd4 4 ♘xd4 a6 5 ♘c3 ♕c7
   6 f4!?
A speciality of Tolnai's. With this move, White usually intends to castle queenside and launch a kingside pawn storm.
   6 ...   b5! *(D)*
Retaining maximum flexibility. 6...d6?! would again disclose Black's formation far too early.

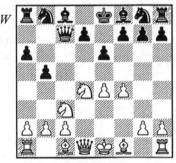

   7 ♗d3
7 a3 is not in the spirit of White's plans and Black can use

the extra tempo to develop his pieces as in Pietzsch-Portisch, Lugano OL 1968: 7...♗b7 8 ♗d3 ♘c6 9 ♘b3 d6 10 0-0 ♘f6 11 ♕e2 ♗e7 12 g4 d5 13 e5 ♘d7 14 ♗e3 g5!.

7 ...   ♗b7

Black tried to dislodge the knight on d4 with 7...♗c5?! but was badly punished after 8 ♘b3 ♗e7 9 ♕g4! b4 10 e5 g6 11 ♘e4 ♗b7 12 ♕e2 f5 13 ♘ed2 ♘c6 14 ♘c4 ♗h4+ 15 g3 ♗e7 16 ♖g1 ♘h6 17 ♗e3 0-0 18 0-0-0 a5 19 ♘b6 ♖ab8 20 ♗xf5 ♘xe5 21 ♖xd7 ♘xd7 22 ♗xe6+ ♖f7 23 ♘xd7 a4 24 ♘bc5 ♗xc5 25 ♗xc5 ♖a8 26 ♗xf7+ ♘xf7 27 ♕e7 ♖c8 28 ♖e1 b3 29 ♕e8+ 1-0 in Smirin-Kurajica, Zagreb Z 1993.

8 ♕f3

8 ♕e2 is a major alternative:

a) 8...♘f6?! 9 e5 ♘d5 10 ♘xd5 ♗xd5 11 0-0 g6 12 a4 b4 13 ♗e3 ♗e7 14 ♘f3 0-0 15 ♘d2 f5 16 ♘c4 ♗xc4 17 ♗xc4 ♗c5 18 b3 g5 19 g3 ♖f7 20 ♗xc5 ♕xc5+ 21 ♕f2 ♕c7 22 ♖ad1 ♘c6 23 ♗e2 ♖g7 24 ♔h1 ♘e7 25 ♗f3 ♖c8 26 ♕d4 gxf4 27 gxf4 ♘g6 28 ♕xb4 ± was Dvoirys-Vyzhmanavin, St. Petersburg Z 1993.

b) Of course, there is no need for Black to play as adventurously as in the above example and he can simply play in a nor-

mal Scheveningen fashion as in Dvoirys-Ribli, Debrecen Echt 1992, which went 8...d6 9 0-0 ♘f6 10 ♔h1 ♘bd7 11 ♗d2 ♗e7 12 ♖ae1 b4 13 ♘a4 ♘c5! 14 ♘xc5 dxc5 15 ♘b3 c4! 16 ♗xc4 ♘xe4 17 f5 exf5 18 ♖xf5 0-0 19 ♗f4 ♗d6 20 ♕f1 ♖ae8 21 ♖d1 g6 22 ♖f6 ♗e5 23 ♗xe5 ♖xe5 24 ♖f4 ♖h5 0-1.

8 ...   ♘f6
9 ♗e3   ♘c6 (D)

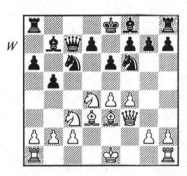

10 0-0-0

Or 10 g4:

a) Van der Wiel-Gheorghiu, Baden 1980 went 10...d6 11 g5 ♘d7 12 0-0-0 ♘c5 13 ♔b1 ♘b4 14 ♕h3 ♘bxd3 15 cxd3 b4 16 ♘ce2 ♕d7 17 ♖hf1 a5 18 ♘c1 ♗e7 19 f5 e5 20 ♘f3 ♘xe4!! 21 ♔a1 ♘c3! 22 bxc3 bxc3 and White's aggressive formation had been reduced to a defensive task.

b) A very interesting alternative to the more normal set-ups was seen in Landa-Tregubov, Russian Ch 1992 which went **10...h5!** 11 g5?! (better is 11 gxh5 ♘xd4 12 ♗xd4 ♘xh5) 11...♘g4 12 ♗g1 ♘xd4 13 ♗xd4 e5! 14 fxe5 ♗c5 15 e6 0-0 16 ♗xc5 ♕xc5 17 exd7 ♕xg5 18 ♕g3 f5 19 h4 ♕h6 20 ♕c7 ♕e3+ 21 ♘e2 ♗xe4 22 ♗xe4 fxe4 23 ♕g3 ♖ad8 24 ♕xe3 ♘xe3 25 ♔d2 ♖f3 26 ♖ae1 ♖xd7+ 27 ♔c1 b4 28 c3 ♖f2 29 cxb4 ♘g2 30 ♖d1 ♖c7+ 31 ♘c3 e3 32 ♖d8+ ♔f7 33 ♔d1 ♖xc3 34 bxc3 e2+ 35 ♔c1 ♖f1+ 0-1.

10	...	b4
11	♘ce2	♘a5
12	g4 *(D)*	

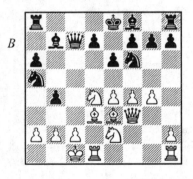

| 12 | ... | d5! |

Yet again, the 'solution' lies in classical chess strategy. Black strikes in the centre in response to a flank attack. **12...d6** is possible but obviously White would

then have a free hand with his kingside attack.

13 e5

The only move, as 13 exd5 ♘xd5 is probably already worse for White.

| 13 | ... | ♘d7 |
| 14 | ♔b1 | |

Polgar gives **14 b3 g5!?** 15 fxg5 ♗g7 16 g6 hxg6 17 ♗xg6 fxg6 (17...♘xe5?! 18 ♘xe6!) 18 ♘xe6 ♕xe5 19 ♘xg7+ ♕xg7 20 ♗d4 ♕h6+ (or 20...♘e5) as being fine for Black.

| 14 | ... | ♘c4 |

Again, **14...g5!?** is a possibility.

| 15 | ♗c1 | 0-0-0 |
| 16 | h4 | |

16 b3 ♘a3+ 17 ♔a1 (17 ♗xa3 bxa3) 17...g5 is given as unclear but obviously Black is extremely active.

16	...	♘c5
17	b3	♘a3+
18	♔a1 *(D)*	

18 ♗xa3 doubles Black's pawns but gives too many mating opportunities on the dark squares.

| 18 | ... | f6? |

A strange decision that weakens Black's solid pawn structure for nothing. Normal in these types of positions is **18...♔b8** intending ...♖c8.

B

19 c3?

White misses his chance to attack Black's weak pawns with **19 ♕e3!** fxe5 20 ♕xe5 (20 fxe5 g5! is good for Black) 20...♗d6 21 ♕e3 ♖he8 22 ♗b2 e5 23 fxe5± as the d4-square is firmly blockaded.

19 ...   fxe5
20 fxe5 (D)

B

20 ...   ♘c4!∓

A clever tactic which wins White's e5-pawn.

21 ♘xe6

21 cxb4 fails to 21...♘xe5: **22 ♕e3** ♘cxd3 23 ♘xe6 ♕d7 24 ♘xd8 d4!∓ or **22 ♕g3** ♘cxd3 23 ♘xe6 ♕e7 (23...♕d7? 24 ♘xd8 ♕xd8 25 ♖xd3 ♘xd3 26 ♕xd3±) 24 ♘xd8 ♘xc1∓ – Polgar.

21 ...   ♘xe5
22 ♕g3

22 ♕f5 is met by 22...g6 23 ♕f6 ♘xe6 24 ♕xe6+ (24 ♕xh8 ♗g7 is winning for Black) 24...♔b8 25 ♗xa6 ♗g7! 26 ♗xb7 ♕xb7 with a winning advantage to Black.

22 ...   ♘xe6
23 ♗f5   ♔b8
24 ♗xe6   bxc3
25 ♘xc3

25 ♗f4 fails to 25...c2 26 ♖d2 ♗d6 27 ♗xd5 ♘g6!.

25 ...   d4
26 ♖hf1

26 ♖he1 ♗b4! is an annoying pin.

26...♗b4 27 ♘a4 ♖he8 28 ♗f5 ♗c6 29 ♗b2 g6 30 ♗b1 ♗xa4 31 bxa4 ♗c3 32 ♗xc3 ♕xc3+ 33 ♕xc3 dxc3 34 ♖c1 ♖c8 35 ♖f4 ♖c5 36 ♖b4+ ♔a7 37 ♖b3 ♖ec8 38 ♗e4 ♖8c7 39 ♖cb1 ♘c6 40 ♗xc6 ♖5xc6 41 ♖b4 ♖c4 42 a3? *(D)*

42 ♖xc4 is better but Black is still winning after 42...♖xc4 43 ♖g1 ♖b4 44 a3 ♖b3 45 ♔a2 ♖b2+ 46 ♔a1 ♖h2∓.

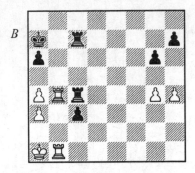

**42...Exb4 43 axb4 Ec4 44 h5?
a5! 45 hxg6 hxg6 46 ⌛a2 Exb4
47 Eg1 c2 48 g5 ⌛b7 0-1**

Black wins after 49 Ec1 Exa4+
50 ⌛b3 Eb4!.

Notes based on analysis by Judit Polgar in *Informator 53*.

Summary

The Scheveningen lines are one of the toughest systems to learn and master. This chapter has shown two types of defence for Black: the relatively new 7...♗c5 and the more conservative approach of 7...♘c6. As I have already mentioned, I personally prefer the newer 7...♗c5 option as this is largely uncharted territory. However, I have occasionally used the ...♘c6 systems and though they are difficult to win with, Black is extremely solid in all lines.

White also has the option of developing his king's bishop to e2 but you are very unlikely to meet this as most players develop the bishop to d3. If you do, 8...♗b4 will be a valuable equalising weapon.

The Tolnai-Polgar game shows how to deal with the less restrained players who treat the Sicilian with no respect whatsoever and play for mate.

5 Early c4 – Maroczy Bind

As explained in the previous chapter, White has found better ways to achieve the Maroczy Bind and hence the move order 1 e4 c5 2 ♘f3 e6 3 d4 cxd4 4 ♘xd4 a6 5 c4 has been superseded by 5 ♗d3 followed by a later c2-c4. Nevertheless, this line is still a major option for White and though Black can often play a simple Hedgehog, the early c2-c4 gives him other options such as the annoying ...♗f8-b4 pin (which White usually avoids by playing a3). The major difference between this form of the Hedgehog and the type arrived at via the main line is that White's light-squared bishop has the option of developing on e2 instead of d3. Black, however, should not be overly concerned about this as this option usually means that White does not launch a kingside attack as his bishop is better placed on d3 for this.

I shall take the starting position of the early c4 lines after the moves 1 e4 c5 2 ♘f3 e6 3 d4 cxd4 4 ♘xd4 a6 5 c4 ♘f6 6 ♘c3 ♕c7 (D).

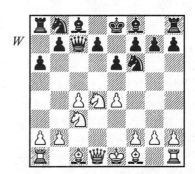

The main move used by White here is 7 ♗d3?!, which after 7...♘c6 transposes to the lines given in the main-line chapter (see Kamsky-I.Gurevich). Thus we have already covered the main option for White and now turn our attention to the lesser but nonetheless quite frequently chosen paths.

Apart from 7 ♗d3?!, White has two other reasonable alternatives in 7 a3!? and 7 ♗e2. The merits of these and some sub-variations will now be discussed in the annotated games.

I will stress once again that as Black, the reader will nowadays rarely meet 5 c4 and thus in some ways this is the least important of the chapters in this book. Nevertheless, chess openings are very much like fashion and older openings may at any time come back from the dead.

Game 27
Hector-Spasov
Chartres 1990

1 e4 c5 2 ♘f3 e6 3 d4 cxd4 4 ♘xd4 a6 5 c4 ♕c7 6 ♗e2 ♘f6
7 ♘c3   ♗b4

Black is by no means forced to play in this manner. Many players prefer to stick to the normal Hedgehog via 7...b6:

a) 8 ♗e3 ♗b7 9 f3 ♗e7 10 ♖c1 0-0 11 ♔f2 ♖d8 12 g4 ♘c6 13 ♘xc6 dxc6 14 ♕g1 c5 15 h4 ♗d6?! (15...♖d4! 16 h5 ♖ad8 17 g5 ♘d7 18 ♕g2 ♘e5 19 ♖hd1 ♖xd1∓ – van der Wiel) 16 h5 ♗f4 17 g5 ♗xe3+ 18 ♔xe3 ♘d7 19 ♕h2 ♘e5 20 h6 g6 21 ♕f4 f5 22 gxf6 ♖d7 23 ♖cd1 ♖c8 24 ♖xd7 ♘xd7 25 ♕xc7 ♖xc7 26 ♖d1 ♔f7 27 ♖d6 ♗c6 28 ♗f1 ♔xf6 29 ♘d5+ ♔e5 30 ♖xd7 1-0 was one game.

b) 8 0-0?! ♗b7 9 ♕d3 (9 f3 ♗d6) 9...d6 10 ♗g5 ♘bd7 11 ♕h3 ♗e7= as in Van der Wiel-Schneider, Leeuwarden 1992.

7...d6?! is playable but yet again unnecessarily committal on Black's part.

8 0-0

This has become the main move since the game Fischer-Portisch, Varna OL 1962 where after 8 ♘c2 ♗xc3+ 9 bxc3 ♘c6 10 f3 0-0 11 ♗a3 ♖d8 12 ♗d6 ♕a5 13 ♘b4 ♘e8 14 0-0 ♘xd6 15 ♕xd6 ♕a3 16 c5 a5 17 ♘xc6 bxc6 18 ♕d4 d5 19 cxd6 ♖xd6 20 ♕b6 h6 21 ♖ad1 ♖xd1 22 ♖xd1 ♕xc3 23 h3 ♕b4 24 ♕c7 ♕b7 25 ♖d8+ ♔h7 26 ♕xb7 ♗xb7 27 ♖d7 ♗a6 28 ♗xa6 ♖xa6 29 ♖xf7 ♔g6, a draw was agreed ten moves later.

8   ...   ♗xc3
9   bxc3   d6
10 ♗a3 *(D)*

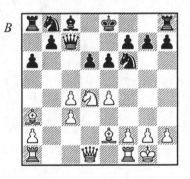

10   ...   ♘xe4
11 ♗f3   ♘c5
12 ♕d2!   ♘bd7

12...0-0 13 ♖fd1 ♖d8 14 ♘b3 and White will regain the pawn and have the two bishops.

13 ♕g5   0-0
14 ♕e7! *(D)*

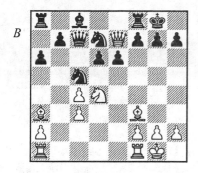

A typical move by White in these lines. Although he has the two bishops, the damage inflicted on his pawn structure is a very big drawback. Thus White must play as actively as possible and pose as many problems for Black as possible.

Black is only a tempo away from completing his development, when his knights will start to dominate the white bishops.

| 14 | ... | ♖a7! |

The only good move. Black could have played **14...♖b8?!** (in order to play ...b6) but the queen would not have been given any protection.

| 15 | ♖ad1 | b6 |
| 16 | ♘c6 | ♘e5! |

The point of 14...♖a7!.

| 17 | ♕xd6 | ♘xf3+ |

17...♘xc4? is too risky in view of 18 ♗xc5! bxc5 (18...♘xd6 19 ♗xd6! ±) 19 ♕xc5 ♘b6 20 ♖d6 ♖b7 21 ♖fd1± – Spasov.

18	gxf3	♕xd6
19	♖xd6	♖c7
20	♖b1	♗b7
21	♖xb6?!	

With this move, White temporarily wins a pawn but his set of doubled pawns actually gives Black the advantage. Better was **21 ♘d4 ♘d7** (21...e5? 22 ♖dxb6 exd4 23 cxd4! ♗xf3 24 ♗xc5 ± or 21...♘a4 22 ♖b4 ♘xc3 23 ♖dxb6 ♗c8 24 ♖b3 ♘a4 25 ♗xf8 ♘xb6 26 c5 ♘d5 27 ♗d6 ♖b7 28 c6 ♖xb3 29 ♘xb3 and White again has the advantage) 22 ♖xd7 ♖xd7 23 ♗xf8 ♔xf8 24 ♖xb6 e5 25 ♘c6 ♖d6 26 ♖xb7 ♖xc6 and a draw is the most likely result – Spasov.

21	...	♘a4
22	♘e5	♘xb6
23	♖xb6	f6
24	♗xf8	♔xf8
25	♘d3	♗xf3
26	c5	

White cannot afford to further open the position with **26 ♖xe6 ♖xc4 27 ♖xa6 ♗e2! 28 ♖a8 ♔e7 29 ♖a7+ ♔d6 30 ♘e1 ♖g4+ 31 ♔h1 ♗b5 intending ...♗c6∓** .

26	...	♔f7
27	♔f1	♗d5
28	♔e2	♗xa2
29	♔e3	

29 ♖xa6? ♗c4 30 ♖d6 (30 ♖a5 ♖d7∓) 30...♖xc5∓.

| 29 | ... | ♗c4 |

30	♘b2	♗f1
31	♔d4	♖d7+
32	♔e3	♔e7
33	c4	♖c7
34	♖xa6	g5
35	♔d4	♗g2
36	♔c3	♖xc5?
37	♖a7+	♔d6
38	♖xh7	♖f5
39	♘d1	♗f1
40	♖a7	♖f3+
41	♘e3?	*(D)*

41 ♔b4! would have given White excellent drawing chances, e.g. **41...♗d3 42 ♖a3!** e5 43 ♘b2! =, **41...♗e2? 42 ♘c3** ♖xf2 43 ♘e4+ ± or **41...♖f4 42** ♖a6+ ♔e5 43 ♘e3!.

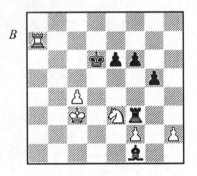

41 ...   f5!
In a race between passed pawns, Black's bishop is far superior to White's knight.

42 ♖a6+ ♔e5 43 ♖a1 ♗h3 44 ♔d3 ♖xf2 45 c5 f4 46 ♘d1 ♗f1+ 47 ♔c3 ♖xh2∓ 48 ♘b2 ♗e2 49 ♖c1 ♔d5 50 ♔b4 ♔c6 51 ♘c4

♗xc4 52 ♔xc4 f3 53 ♖e1 ♖e2 **0-1**

A typical game in this variation. Black grabs the pawn in the opening and weathers the storm to a better endgame thanks to his better pawn structure.

I would personally still play a pure Hedgehog against the early c4 variations but modern theory does recommend 7...♗b4! as the 'antidote' to White's system.

Game 28
Torre-Karpov
Bad Lauterberg 1977

1 e4 c5 2 ♘f3 e6 3 d4 cxd4 4 ♘xd4 a6 5 c4 ♕c7

6 a3
One of the main moves in the early c4 lines. 6 a3 prevents the annoying pin ...♗b4 and at the same time puts the onus on Black to reveal his favoured formation.

6 ...   ♘f6
7 ♘c3   ♘c6!?
7...d6 is perhaps more viable than in pervious examples as in Velimirović-Abramović, Stara Pazova 1988, which continued 8 ♗e3 ♗e7 9 ♖c1 0-0 10 g4 ♘c6 11 g5 ♘d7 12 ♘xc6 bxc6 13 f4 c5 14 ♗d3 ♖e8 15 0-0 ♗b7 16 ♖f3 ♗f8 17 h4 g6 18 h5 ♗g7 19 ♖h3 d5!?.

8 ♗e3

White can gain a slight concession with **8 ♘xc6 dxc6 9 ♗e2**
since in similar positions this
bishop has already been developed on the less useful d3-square.
However, this in no way im-
proves his chances of playing for
an advantage and does not 'repair' the weakness on d4.

    8 ...   **♗e7**
    9 ♖c1   **♘e5**
    10 ♗e2   **♘g6**
    11 0-0 *(D)*

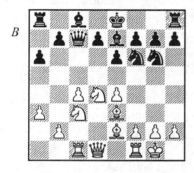

11 ...   **b6**

Keeping the b8-h2 diagonal
open for as long as possible. Karpov describes the merits of this
ploy:

"There is a good reason behind
this developing plan. Black
leaves his d-pawn on its original
square, which allows him to create an illusion of counterplay
along the b8-h2 diagonal and on
the kingside, but more important

is the fact that his e-pawn on e6
is not weakened and therefore the
advance of White's f-pawn, f2-
f4-f5, is not dangerous. Mean-
time, Black has been able to defend against a queenside squeeze
by c4-c5 and White cannot ex-
ploit the fact that Black has left
the king in the centre." – from
My Best Games by Karpov.

A perfect explanation of one of
the most important concepts in
the Kan, the b8-h2 diagonal.

    12 f4   **0-0**
    13 b4   **♗b7**
    14 ♗d3   **♖ac8**
    15 ♘b3 *(D)*

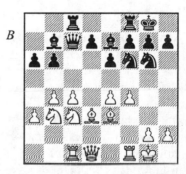

15 ...   **d6**

It would have been dangerous
to further delay this inevitable
move. White is threatening the
simple ♘a4, winning the b6-
pawn and also has set up the possibility of c4-c5.

    16 ♕e2   **♖fe8**
    17 h3   **♘d7**

The first of many knight hops. Karpov decides to use the f6-square for his bishop.

18 ♕f2   ♗a8
19 ♖c2   ♕b8
20 ♖fc1   ♗h4 (D)

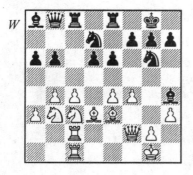

21 g3?!

At a critical juncture, White decides to fulfil his first move advantage. The weakness along the a8-h1 diagonal not a serious weakness on its own but as Karpov mentions, it gives Torre the wrong idea as he decides to start an ambitious kingside attack.

In fact this is a typical Hedgehog game in that Black teases White to come forward when a more solid option would have retained the advantage. In this case, the simple **21 ♕d2** would have retained an edge. Nevertheless, Black take heart from the fact that even if White had decided to play the more solid option, the day

will eventually arrive when White will inevitably lose patience and go for the win. It is thus of utmost importance that Black is ready with his best defensive formation at all times.

21 ...   ♗d8
22 ♘d2   ♗f6

I again quote Karpov:

"It is quite difficult to comment on all these manoeuvres, because they are only general preparations. Yet, since nobody has had chosen any positive plan, this waiting game plays a very important part. What kind of a plan should one choose anyway? A break on the queenside? A kingside attack? Or perhaps just keep the balance in the centre and wait? Well, all this depends on the character and taste of a chess player."

A perfect description of doing nothing constructively!

23 h4   h6

Karpov foregoes the possibility of **23...♗xc3 24 ♖xc3 ♘f6** when the simple **25 ♗e2** would retain the bishop.

24 h5   ♘gf8
25 g4?!

Finally Black makes his choice – but the wrong choice as Black's pieces are perfectly placed for the pawn storm.

25 ...   ♘h7

26 e5

After his dubious 25th move, White really had no choice but to continue in this fashion. Given one more move, Black would have played the thematic thrust in the centre (the classic counterattack to a wing attack), ...e5!. Of course, 27 f5? is simply met by 27...♗g5, followed by ...♘f6 with a massive positional advantage to Black.

26	...	dxe5
27	g5	exf4
28	♗xf4	♗e5
29	g6	fxg6
30	hxg6	♗xf4
31	gxh7+	♔h8
32	♖f1	♖f8
33	♗e4	♘e5
34	♕g2	♘xc4

0-1

Notes based on Karpov's analysis in *My Best Games*.

The following annotated game is not of much theoretical value but it highlights one of Black's lesser-known themes in this variation.

Game 29
Ehlvest-Kasparov
Linares 1991

1 e4 c5 2 ♘f3 e6 3 d4 cxd4 4 ♘xd4 a6 5 c4 ♘f6 6 ♘c3 ♕c7 7 ♗d3 *(D)*

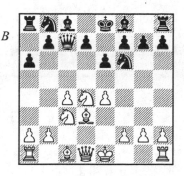

7 ...   ♗e7?

A dubious novelty by Kasparov. From previous games we know that 7...♘c6! gives Black a good game. Nevertheless, the game is still highly instructive in highlighting one of the lesser-known themes of the Sicilian.

8 f4!   d6

White correctly capitalises on Black's dubious seventh move by forcing ...d6. It is important for Black to avoid committing his minor pieces early as White will then have a free hand in setting up the most dangerous configuration.

9 ♕e2!

The exclamation mark is not for the strength of the move but more for the correctness of White's play in response to Black's early committal play. It is only now that we realise why White is eager to deploy the light-squared bishop on d3 rather than e2. White has the simple idea of playing e4-e5 as quickly as possible, thereby allowing the bishop on d3 to become a major attacking force.

If Black again chooses to be inflexible by committing his king too early by **9...0-0** then White can drum up a huge kingside attack with **10 e5** dxe5 11 fxe5 ♘fd7 12 ♗f4! when all of White's pieces are ready to deliver checkmate.

As Kasparov points out in his *Informator* analysis, **10 ♗e3** is also good for a slight advantage.

9 ...   ♘c6

Protecting e5 but setting up the possibility of another attacking theme.

10 ♘f3!

Continuing the policy of playing for e5. **10 ♘xc6** bxc6 is also good for White.

10 ...   ♘d7

11 a3?

A waste of a move. White should have continued more energetically according to Kasparov via **11 ♗e3** ♘c5 12 ♗c2 b6 13 ♖c1 ♗f6 14 ♗b1! when Black is hanging on but White's harmonious pieces give him a clear edge.

11 ...   ♗f6

12 ♗e3?! *(D)* ♗xc3+!

13 bxc3   e5!

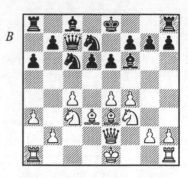

B

Given the outcome of this game, White would have done better to play 12 ♗d2 though most of his early opening advantage has vanished. After this bold exchange of bishop for knight, the game strongly resembles a Nimzo-Indian Defence in which Black also exchanges his dark-squared bishop for a knight in return for a better pawn structure.

With 13...e5, Kasparov further limits the scope of White's two bishops.

14 f5 *(D)*

A difficult decision as after **14 0-0** exf4 15 ♗xf4 ♘ce5 Black is again blockading and the two bishops are clearly inferior to the two knights.

14 ...   ♘cb8!!

A fantastic move, which shows the need for experience in all types of positions. After White has completely blockaded the position with 14 f5, it is safe for

Black to 'undevelop' in this fashion for a superior set-up.

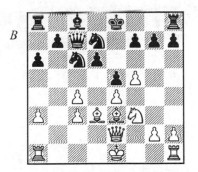

The above diagram is a fine example of what Black is trying to achieve in a slightly different variation of the Kan arising from the move order 1 e4 c5 2 ♘f3 e6 3 d4 cxd4 4 ♘xd4 a6 5 c4 ♘f6 6 ♘c3 ♕c7 7 ♗e2 ♗b4. An example of the problems that Black can sometimes face in this line can be seen in the game Chandler-Gheorghiu, Surakarta 1982 which continued 8 ♘c2 ♗xc3+ 9 bxc3 ♘c6 10 ♕d3 0-0 11 ♗a3 ♖d8 12 ♗d6 ♕a5 13 ♘b4 ♘e8 14 0-0 b6 15 ♗c7!! ♘e5 16 ♗xe5 ♕xe5 17 ♘c6 ♕c7 18 ♘xd8 ♕xd8 19 ♖ab1 ♗b7 20 ♖fd1 ♗c6 21 e5 b5 22 cxb5 axb5 23 ♗f3 ♗xf3 with a winning position for White.

15 0-0

15 ♕f2 ♘f6 16 ♕g3 ♘bd7 17 ♕xg7 ♖g8 18 ♕h6 ♘g4 19 ♕xh7 ♘df6 20 ♕h4 ♘xe3 21 ♕xf6

♘xg2+ 22 ♔d2 ♕b6 with a dangerous attack for Black - Kasparov.

15	...	♘c5
16	♗c2	♘bd7
17	♖fd1	♘f6
18	♘d2	

White would gain nothing by doubling Black's pawns with 18 ♗g5 ♗d7 19 ♗xf6 gxf6 as Black's structure is still superior to White's and the open g-file can also be used as part of a kingside attack.

18	...	♗d7
19	♗g5	♗c6
20	♕f3	0-0-0
21	♖e1	h6
22	♗h4 *(D)*	

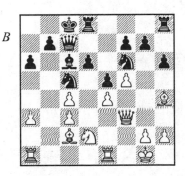

22 ... ♖dg8!

The only way to progress. Black's superior pawn structure is not enough to win the game. Kasparov must open another front on the kingside.

23 ♔h1?

23 ♘f1 ♘h7! 24 ♕g4 ♔b8 25 ♘e3 g5 26 fxg6 fxg6 27 ♖f1 h5 and though White has finally managed to re-route his knight to e3, Black will simply capture the white knight when it finally lands on d5.

23	...	♘fd7
24	♘f1	g5
25	♗f2	h5
26	♕d1	h4
27	♕b1	♘f6
28	♗xc5?	

White's patience finally snaps and he wrongly breaks out. More stubborn was 28 ♘d2 with a clear advantage to Black.

28	...	dxc5
29	♘e3	♕a5!∓
30	♕b2 *(D)*	

30	...	h3
31	g3	♘xe4
32	♗xe4	♗xe4+
33	♔g1	♖d8
34	♘g4	♗xf5
35	♘xe5	♕c7?!
36	♕f2	♗e6
37	♖ab1?!	♖d6
38	♖b2	♖hd8
39	♖be2	f6
40	♘g6	♗xc4

0-1

White had seen enough.

Summary:

In many respects, this chapter is the most 'redundant' in the survey. The early c4 lines have been superseded by the main lines and Black can always play a simple Hedgehog anyway.

6   Miscellaneous systems

This chapter will deal with two of White's systems which are not frequently seen in grandmaster chess but are reasonably popular in all levels below. The two systems are:

A: 1 e4 c5 2 ♘f3 e6 3 d4 cxd4 4 ♘xd4 a6 5 ♘c3 ♕c7 6 g3
B: 1 e4 c5 2 ♘f3 e6 3 b3!?

A: 6 g3

These g3 systems are closely related to the Closed Sicilian with the difference that White has opened the c-file by playing d2-d4 whereas in the Closed Sicilian, the pawn is played to d3. Thus the ideas in these systems are a mixture of Open Sicilian concepts (play along the semi-open c- and d-files) and Closed Sicilian / King's Indian Attack formations.

Armed with some knowledge of the current main line, Black is currently considered to be doing fine in these lines and has nothing to fear.

Game 30
Porubski-I.Gurevich
Saint Martin 1993

1 e4 c5 2 ♘f3 e6 3 d4 cxd4 4 ♘xd4 a6 5 ♘c3 ♕c7 6 g3 *(D)*

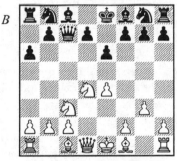

6 ...   ♗b4!?
This is currently considered the main line of this variation. Black immediately challenges White's set-up and forces either 7 ♘c2 or ♗d2 – both of which White would not play in normal circumstances.

7 ♗d2
7 ♘e2 is discussed in the next annotated game.

7 ...   ♘f6
7...♘c6?! does not work well at this stage in conjunction with 6...♗b4, e.g. 8 ♘xc6 and then:

a) **8...dxc6** 9 ♕g4! ♗f8 10 f4
♘f6 11 ♕f3 e5 12 f5 b5 13 g4 h6
14 h4 ♗b7 15 ♖h3! 0-0-0 16 g5
♘d7 17 0-0-0 with advantage to
White as in Barlov-Kovačević,
Torcy 1991.

b) Black got away with
8...bxc6?! in Vasiukov-Panno,
Moscow GMA 1989 after 9 ♕g4
♗f8 10 ♕e2 d6 11 ♗g2 ♘f6 because White continued with the
ambitious **12 g4?!** e5! 13 g5 ♘d7
14 h4 ♘c5 15 0-0-0 ♘e6 16 ♗h3
♗e7 17 f4 exf4 18 ♕h2 0-0 19
♗xf4 ♘xf4 20 ♕xf4 ♕a5 21
♗xc8 ♖axc8 22 ♖d4 ♖b8 23 ♖a4
♕c5 but instead the simple **12 f4**
followed by g4 would be good for
White.

8 ♗g2   ♗e7

The bishop has done its job of
disrupting White's development
flow and now returns to its best
square, e7. A major alternative is
8...♘c6 but Sicilian players are
likely to avoid this option as the
position loses its Sicilian 'feel'.
Practical examples after **9 ♘xc6**
include:

a) **9...bxc6?!** 10 0-0 ♗e7 11
♖e1 e5 12 ♘a4 d6 13 c4 ♗e6 14
c5! ± as in Diaz-Portisch, Biel IZ
1976. 9...bxc6?! is now very
rarely seen and has been superseded by 9...dxc6.

b) **9...dxc6** 10 0-0 0-0 11 f4
♖d8 12 ♕e2 b5 13 ♖ad1 ♗b7 14
a3 ♗f8 15 e5 ♘d5 16 ♘e4 c5 17
c4 ♘e7 18 ♘d6 ♗xg2 19 ♕xg2
♘f5 20 ♘xf5 exf5 21 ♕e2 ♖ab8
22 ♗c1 ♖d4 23 cxb5 axb5 24
♗e3 ♖e4 25 ♕d2 with a slight
advantage to Black in Popović-
Cvitan, Vršac 1987.

Both 9 ♘ce2?! and 9 ♘b3?!
have been played but it is clear
that Black gains a tempo for nothing and the knight on d4 is driven
away free of charge.

9 0-0

An interesting alternative was
seen in Tarjan-Commons, US Ch
1975 when White played **9 g4!?**
d6 10 g5 ♘fd7 11 f4 ♘c6 12
♘xc6 bxc6 13 0-0 d5 and according to *Informator 21*, the position
is unclear.

9 ...   0-0
10 h3   ♘c6
11 ♗e3   ♘e5
12 ♘de2   d6

The immediate **12...♘c4?!** is
premature as after 13 ♗c1 followed by b2-b3, Black has
gained nothing.

13 a4   ♖b8
14 ♗a7   ♖a8
15 ♗e3   b6 *(D)*
16 g4

A thematic move in these and
many other King's Indian Attack
type positions. White expands on
the kingside for positional as well
as tactical reasons.

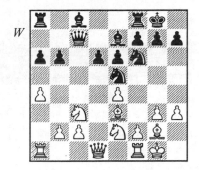

Positionally, the thrust g4-g5 will increase White's control over d5. Tactically, White sets up the possibility of a kingside pawn storm with f2-f4 and g4-g5. In addition, the g3-square is vacated for the knight on e2.

16 ...   ♗b7
17 ♗d4   ♖fd8!

An unusual place for the king's rook but the beginning of a thematic plan in which Black strikes in the centre.

18 f4   ♘c6
19 ♗e3 *(D)*

19 ...   d5!

A common theme in this book where one side counterattacks in the centre in reaction to a flank attack. It is important that Black takes advantage of the congestion in White's position. If given the chance, White will play ♘g3, ♕e2 and ♖ad1 with an undisputed spatial advantage.

20 exd5

Better was 20 e5 though Black can still present considerable difficulties after 20...♘e4! and Black has no clear way to reorganise and establish control over the position. If 21 ♘xe4 then Black has the initiative after 21...dxe4 22 ♕e1 ♘b4! 23 ♘d4 (23 ♖c1? ♘d5! intending ...e3 ∓) 23...♖xd4 24 ♗xd4 ♘xc2 25 ♖c1 ♗c5!.

20 ...   ♘b4!

Of course, Black does not immediately recapture and leave himself with an isolated pawn. It is far better to keep the d-file open when White's weaknesses on the kingside will begin to count.

21 ♕c1   ♘fxd5
22 ♘xd5   ♗xd5
23 ♗xd5   ♘xd5
24 ♗d4   ♕c4
25 ♖f2   b5!

A move played in anticipation of c2-c3 by White in which case ...b5-b4 will undermine White's pawn base. Also possible was 25...♖ac8 26 c3 ♕d3 27 ♕f1 ♘e3 28 ♖f3 ♕xd4 29 ♘xd4 ♘xf1 30 ♔xf1 ♗f6, when Black is still better but White's chances of drawing are improved.

26	b3	♕c6
27	♕b2	♘f6
28	♔h2	♖ac8
29	c3	♘e4
30	♖ff1 *(D)*	

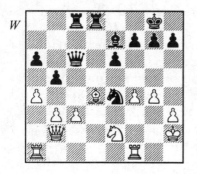

| 30 | ... | ♗d6! ∓ |

White now has no hiding place for his king as each diagonal is controlled by either the black queen or the bishop.

31	axb5	axb5
32	♖ac1	♘g5
33	♔g3	f6
34	c4	bxc4
35	♖xc4	♕e4
36	♖c3?	

A blunder, though even after 36 ♕c1 ♖b8 37 ♕d1 e5! White's position is falling apart.

36	...	♖xc3+
37	♕xc3	♕xe2
38	♖e1	♘e4+
	0-1	

A typical game in this variation. Black waits for the inevitable g4 and immediately breaks in the centre with ...d5!, liberating his entire army.

The next game discusses White's other 7th move option, 7 ♘e2 instead of 7 ♗d2. However, as the reader shall see, the two lines are extremely similar and often result in the same type of position.

Game 31
Ye Jiangchuan-Zapata
Manila OL 1992

1 e4 c5 2 ♘f3 e6 3 d4 cxd4 4 ♘xd4 a6 5 ♘c3 ♕c7 6 g3 ♗b4 *(D)*

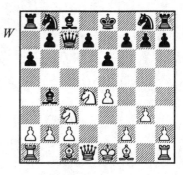

7 ♘e2

The previous game saw 7 ♗d2 but the two moves are interchangeable in that White will invariably drop the knight back from d4 to e2.

7 ...   ♗e7

An early retreat though it makes little or no difference as both sides have a standard plan to follow. 7...♘f6 8 ♗g2 is an alternative:

a) Black delayed ...♗e7 for slightly too long in Malishauskas-J.Polgar, Biel IZ 1993 with 8...♘c6!? 9 ♗f4! ♕a5 10 a3 ♗e7 11 b4 ♕d8 12 ♘d5 exd5 13 exd5 0-0 14 d6 ♖e8 15 dxe7 ♕xe7 16 ♗f3 d5 17 0-0 ♗f5 and though Malishauskas considers the position to be unclear, I would say that White has a definite advantage.

b) Slightly more accurate was Malishauskas-Urday, Oviedo rpd 1993, which went 8...♗e7! 9 0-0 ♘c6 10 h3 b5 11 f4 d6 12 g4 ♘d7 13 ♘g3 0-0 14 g5 ♖e8 15 f5 ♗f8 16 f6 g6 17 h4 ♗b7 18 h5 ♘de5 19 hxg6 fxg6 20 ♘ce2 ♘d8! and the position was dynamically balanced.

8	a4!?	♘f6
9	♗g2	♘c6
10	0-0	0-0
11	h3	♖b8
12	g4	d6
13	♘g3 (D)	

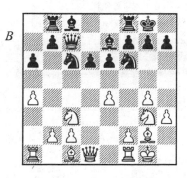

13 ...   b5

In contrast to the last game, Black expands in the normal Sicilian fashion with ...b5. Black's plan is very simple: advance the b-pawn to b4 thereby dislodging the white knight from c3 and then apply pressure to the c2-pawn along the open c-file. White, of course, will be attempting to storm Black's kingside fortress with f4, g5 and f5.

14	axb5	axb5
15	g5	♘d7
16	f4	♖e8
17	♔h1	♗f8
18	f5!?	

Ye Jiangchuan points out 18 ♘ce2!? with the idea of b3 and ♗b2 though after 18...♘b4! 19 c3 ♘c6, White can no longer develop his bishop on the long diagonal and Black also has the threat of ...b5-b4. The text move is a big concession by White who forever gives up the e5-square to Black. In return, however, he has excellent attacking chances against the black king.

18	...	♘ce5
19	♘ce2	g6
20	♘d4	

20 ♘f4!? would have helped White's attack and at the same time kept an eye over d5.

20	...	♗g7
21	h4	♘c5
22	h5	b4!

Black has maximised the defence around his king's position with the manoeuvre ...♗f8-g7 and now launches his 'distraction' on the queenside.

23 f6

Also possible was 23 h6!? ♗f8 24 b3 with a similar position to the actual game.

23	...	♗f8
24	b3 *(D)*	

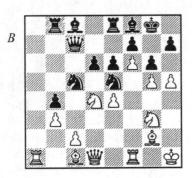

24 ... d5?!

The right idea though the execution and the timing of the break are wrong. A better option was

24...♗b7 though admittedly White has an advantage after 25 ♗f4, making it hard for Black to play ...d5 due to the bishop's indirect attack against the black queen.

25 exd5?

Better was 25 ♗f4! dxe4 (25...♗d6 26 ♕e2! ±) 26 hxg6 hxg6 27 ♘c6! ♕xc6 28 ♗xe5 ♖b5!? 29 ♖a7! ♕b6 30 ♖xf7! ♔xf7 31 ♕g4 intending ♕h3, ♕h7+ Ye Jiangchuan.

25	...	exd5
26	♗f4	♗d6
27	hxg6	hxg6
28	♕e2!	

28 ♕d2 ♗a6! 29 ♖xa6+ ♘xa6 30 ♗xd5 ♕d7! ∓. The text move denies Black the useful a6-f1 diagonal.

28	...	♗g4
29	♕d2! *(D)*	

29 ... ♘f3+!

The only move that keeps Black's game ticking. 29...♘e4 30 ♘xe4 dxe4 31 ♖ae1! or

29...♘ed3 30 ♗xd6 ♕xd6 31
♘ge2! and White is clearly better
in both cases.

30	♗xd6	♕xd6
31	♗xf3	♕xg3
32	♕h2+	♗xf3+
33	♖xf3	♖e1+
34	♖f1	♖xf1+
35	♖xf1	♕xh2+
36	♔xh2	

White has a slight advantage in
this endgame thanks to his pawns
on the kingside which imprison
the black king. However, Black
can create counterplay by attacking these pawns and liquidating
to a worse but drawn rook and
pawn endgame.

36	...	♖e8!
37	♖a1	♘e4
38	♘c6	♘xg5
39	♘e7+	♔h8!
40	♖a4?!	

The only way to keep the game
going was by 40 ♖h1! ♖d8 41
♔g3+ ♘h7 42 ♔f4 ♖d6 43 ♔e5
♖e6+ 44 ♔xd5 ♖xf6 45 ♘c6
when material is equal but
White's better placed king will
aid the cause of his passed pawns.

40...♖d8 41 ♖xb4 d4! 42 ♖b6
♔h7 43 b4 ♘e4 44 b5 ♖d7 45
♘c6= ♘xf6 46 ♘e5 ♖e7 47 ♖xf6
♖xe5 48 ♖xf7+ ½-½

From the two annotated games,
the reader will notice that the

only theory that is needed is
6...♗b4 and the correct timing of
the retreat of this bishop to e7.
Other than that, the standard Sicilian plans of queenside expansion, the ...e5 or ...d5 break all
apply in these positions and previous chapters should be of benefit even here.

System B

This surprisingly popular system is nothing more than White
simply avoiding learning main-
line theory. This may seem a
slightly sweeping statement but
very often, positions in this system transpose to a Maroczy Bind
or Hedgehog structure. In the
main line, White can force Black
into this without actually know-
ing any theory whatsoever and
therefore I do not consider this
system to be dangerous for
Black.

Nevertheless, for the sake of
completeness if nothing else, I
have annotated one game with
this line. It should be noted that
Black has many defensive
structures to choose from and
perhaps the worst one is seen in
the annotated game! Still, the
game does highlight a spectacular resource which is very rarely
seen.

Game 32
Collinson-Mortazavi
Guildford (Smith and Williamson) 1992

1 e4 c5 2 ♘f3 e6
3 b3 *(D)*

3 ... b6!?
Major alternatives include:

a) **3...d6**:

a1) **4 ♗b2 ♘f6 5 ♗b5+ ♘bd7**
6 e5 dxe5 7 ♘xe5 ♗e7 8 0-0 0-0
9 f4 ♕c7 10 ♕f3 a6 11 ♗xd7
♗xd7 12 d3 ♖ad8 13 ♘d2 ♗c8
14 a4 ♘d5 15 ♘e4 f6 16 ♕g3 b5!
∓ as in Chandler-Zapata, Palma
de Mallorca 1989.

a1) **4 d4 cxd4 5 ♘xd4 ♘f6 6**
♗d3 ♗e7 7 0-0 0-0 8 c4 ♗d7 9
♗b2 ♘c6 10 ♘xc6 ♗xc6 11 ♘c3
a6 12 ♕e2 ♖b8 13 ♖ad1 ♕a5 14
♘d5 ♗xd5 15 exd5 e5 16 f4 ♖fe8
17 ♗b1 e4 18 ♖fe1 b5 19 c5 dxc5
20 d6 ♗d8 21 d7 ♖f8 22 ♗xe4 as
in Collinson-Lesiège, Oakham
1992.

b) **3...♘c6 4 ♗b2** and then:

b1) **4...♘f6 5 e5 ♘d5** was seen
in Majerić-Landa, Zagreb 1990,
which continued 6 ♗b5 ♕c7!? 7
0-0 a6 8 ♗xc6 ♕xc6 9 ♖e1 b5 10
d3 ♗b7 11 ♘bd2 ♗e7 12 c4 ♘f4
13 ♘e4 0-0 which is given as
equal by Landa though I prefer
Black due to his two bishops.

b1) Black was a little too ambitious in Bus-Livshits, Oakham
1992 with **4...d5!?** 5 exd5 exd5 6
d4 ♘f6 7 ♗e2 ♗d6 8 0-0 0-0 9
♘c3 a6 10 dxc5 ♗xc5 11 ♘a4
♗a7 12 ♘d4 ♗d7 13 ♘xc6 ♗xc6
14 ♗d4 ♖e8 15 ♗xa7 ♖xa7 16
♕d4 ♖xe2?! 17 ♕xa7 d4 18 ♖fe1
♕d5 19 ♕b8+ ♘e8 20 ♕g3 ±.

c) A move I like is **3...a6!?** as it
puts the onus on White to reveal
his formation before Black. After
4 ♗b2 examples include:

c1) **4...d6 5 g3 b5 6 ♗g2 ♗b7**
7 d3 ♘f6 8 0-0 ♗e7 9 ♘bd2 0-0
10 ♕e2 ♘fd7 11 c3 ♘c6 12 d4
b4 13 d5?! bxc3 14 ♗xc3 exd5 15
exd5 ♘b4 16 ♘c4?! ♘xd5 17
♗a5 ♕b8 18 ♖ad1 ♖e8 19 ♕d2
♘7f6 ∓ Ambrož-Erdelyi, Bern
1992.

c2) **4...♘c6 5 e5 d5 6 exd6 ♘f6**
7 g3 ♗xd6 8 ♗g2 0-0 9 0-0 ♖b8
10 a4 b5 11 axb5 axb5 12 d4 ♗b7
13 dxc5 ♗xc5 14 ♕e2 ♕b6 15
♗xf6 gxf6 16 ♘bd2 ♗e7 17 g4
♘b4 18 ♘e1 ♕d4 19 ♖d1 ♖fd8
20 ♗xb7 ♖xb7 21 ♘g2 ♖bd7

was Odeev-Oratovsky, Jurmala 1989 when Black's control of the d-file gave him a clear advantage.

d) One 'natural' move, which I would advise against, is **3...♘f6?!** which I believe gives White at least the hope for an advantage. After **4 e5 ♘d5 5 ♗b2 ♘c6** practical examples include:

d1) **6 g3 ♗e7 7 c4!? ♘c7 8 ♗g2 0-0 9 0-0 d5?! 10 d4 dxc4 11 bxc4 cxd4 12 ♘xd4 ♘xe5 13 ♕e2** and White has an edge.

d2) Ambrož-Wyss, Bern 1993 saw **6 ♗b5 ♗e7 7 0-0 ♕c7 8 ♗xc6 ♕xc6 9 d4 b5 10 dxc5 ♗xc5 11 ♘bd2 ♘f4 12 ♖e1 ♗b7 13 ♘e4 0-0 14 ♕d2 ♘g6 15 ♖ac1 ♖ac8 16 c4 b4 17 ♖cd1 ♖cd8 18 h4 a6 19 h5 ♘e7 20 h6 g6 21 ♗d4** and Black rather prematurely resigned though he will very shortly be mated on the dark squares.

e) **3...d5 4 exd5 exd5** has been played, but few players enjoy defending the IQP and therefore this line has been all but abandoned:

e1) **5 ♗b2 ♘f6 6 ♗e2 ♗e7 7 0-0 0-0 8 d4 ♘c6 9 ♘c3 ♘e4 10 ♘a4 ♗f6 11 ♖b1 b6 12 ♗b5 ♗b7 13 dxc5 ♗xb2 14 ♖xb2 bxc5 15 ♘d2 ♕a5 16 ♘xe4 dxe4 17 c4 ♖ad8 18 ♕h5** gave White a clear advantage in Westerinen-Ligterink, Wijk aan Zee 1976.

e1) Rozentalis-Dzhandzhgava, Vilnius 1988 saw **5 ♗b5+ ♗d7 6 ♗xd7+ ♘xd7 7 0-0 ♗d6 8 d4 ♘e7 9 ♘c3 h6 10 dxc5 ♘xc5 11 g3 ♗c7 12 ♗a3 b6 13 ♕d4 0-0 14 ♖ad1 ♘e6 15 ♕d3 ♗d6 16 ♗b2 ♘c7 17 ♖fe1 ♕c8 18 ♖e2 ♖d8 19 ♖de1** and though the game was drawn in 33 moves, White always retained the better winning chances and Black was struggling.

> **4 ♗b2   ♗b7**
> **5 ♘c3   d6?!**

Inconsistent with retaining flexibility – and also a bad move! After **5...a6!**, Black can reach the desired Scheveningen positions I was trying to reach where White's bishop is on b2. Then **6 d4 cxd4 7 ♘xd4 ♕c7 8 ♗d3 ♗b4 9 ♘de2 ♘f6 10 0-0 ♘g4 11 g3 ♘c6 12 a3 ♗e7 13 ♘f4 ♘ce5 14 ♗e2 ♘f6 15 ♘d3 ♘g6 16 ♗f3 0-0 17 ♖e1 d6 =** was Velička-Fogarasi, Budapest 1993.

> **6 d4   cxd4 *(D)***

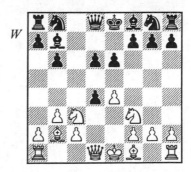

7 ♘xd4?!

In the same tournament, I merrily played down this line in a later game but White had a massive improvement to the game with 7 ♗b5+! ♘d7 8 ♕xd4 intending 0-0-0 and White has a huge lead in development.

7 ...	♘f6
8 ♗b5+	♘bd7
9 ♕e2	a6
10 ♗c6	♗xc6
11 ♘xc6	♕c7
12 ♘b4	

Better was **12 ♘d4** when the position is unclear after 12...e5!? 13 ♘f5 d5! 14 ♘xd5 ♘xd5 15 exd5 ♗b4+ 16 ♔f1 ♗c3! with compensation for the pawn. However, White thought that he could maintain a small edge after 12...d5 13 ♘d3 but he missed Black's spectacular reply.

12 ...	d5
13 ♘d3 *(D)*	

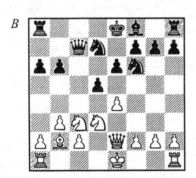

13 ... ♗a3!!

A very strange tactic which solves all of Black's opening problems in one go. The bishop is developed with tempo and White's development is seriously hampered.

14 ♕e3!

The best move. 14 ♘xd5 fails to 14...exd5 15 exd5+ ♔d8! and ...♖e8 winning the queen. 14 0-0-0 ♕xc3! 15 ♗xa3 ♕a1+ 16 ♔d2 ♘xe4 or 14 ♕d2 ♗xb2 15 ♘xb2 ♖c8! and Black wins a pawn.

14 ...	♖c8!
15 ♘xd5	exd5
16 ♗xa3	♕c3+
17 ♔e2	dxe4
18 ♖hc1 *(D)*	

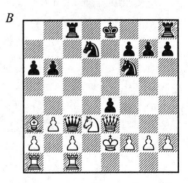

18 ... ♕a5!

White must not be allowed to reorganise his defences and re-route his king to safety.

19	♗b4	♕h5+
20	♔e1	♕xh2
21	♘f4	g5!
22	♘h3	♕xg2
23	♘xg5	♖g8

| 24 | ♘h3 | ♘d5! |

0-1

Clearly the 3 b3 lines are rather unexplored but I feel that in all lines, Black has very little to fear.

Index of Variations